Europe Views America

A CRITICAL EVALUATION

Europe Views America

A CRITICAL EVALUATION

By Edward W. Chester

**Foreword by Mark A. May, Chairman,
U.S. Advisory Commission on Information**

Public Affairs Press, Washington, D. C.

FOREWORD

The author of this book has rendered a useful service by analyzing views and opinions about the United States expressed by European thinkers since the close of World War I. His main thesis is that current criticisms are clearly related to and in some ways based on prior views and attitudes. An appropriate sub-title might be "Forty Years of European Thought About the United States."

The book provides a wealth of background material against which current criticisms by European philosophers, social scientists, and journalists can be evaluated. For example, the question of the prestige of the United States is seen in a new light. Also the focus of attention on comparisons between Russia and the United States is responsible, to a considerable extent, for a loss of historical perspective.

Toward the end of the book there is a chapter which contrasts views of Americans with those of Europeans. This brings into sharp focus what has been called the *distorted image:* the misinterpretation of our history, and misconceptions of our political, economic, and cultural life. What could or should be done about this is naturally not discussed in a historical study; neither does it deal with the troublesome question of the sources of the opinions and views of Europeans. The author does, however, refer to "conscious and unconscious prejudices which contribute to tension between the Old World and the New." This has a direct bearing on the extent to which both sides can accept and profit by frank and friendly criticism of each other.

This book provides valuable background reading for all who are concerned with promoting mutual understanding. It emphasizes the fact that changes in opinions and attitudes occur gradually and that programs designed for affecting such changes must be long-ranged.

MARK A. MAY

Yale University,
New Haven, Conn.

CONTENTS

INTRODUCTION

Had this study appeared in print several years ago, it probably would have been treated as an interesting but largely academic work. While Americans were aware that Europeans and other foreigners had opinions about the United States, they were generally indifferent to what overseas commentators had to say so long as they refrained from being too critical. While we did flare up when some overly hostile analyst took us to task, our resentment was usually of short duration, as we soon turned our attention to more important matters. We did feel a bit uncomfortable in that we were not especially liked abroad, but we tended to dismiss this minor detail on the grounds that foreigners were envious because we were superior to them. There was no doubt in our minds but that the remainder of the free world regarded us as their leader, so we saw no reason for alarm when an occasional diatribe was levelled in our direction.

Today the situation is quite different, since the events of the last year and a half have demonstrated that what the rest of the globe thinks of us is not only important, but probably the most consequential factor which we must deal with in formulating foreign policy. As a result, the present volume is of considerable significance, as it represents the first comprehensive analysis of recent European attitudes towards the United States. Admittedly half-informed analysts have spewed out dozens upon dozens of articles and tracts dealing with trans-Atlantic opinions, but the pretentions of these efforts are usually only matched by their glib distortions and facile inaccuracies. This study, on the other hand, is the result of innumerable hours of research and writing, and thus must not be prejudged as the typical slap-dash affair concocted to meet the need for a book.

The material presented in these pages which reflects unfavorably on the United States should be of especial interest to Americans, since it is an indisputable fact that the Kennedy Administration is highly concerned about the adverse judgments which are currently being directed against us abroad. Such a concern, moreover, is quite justified, as American scientific, social, economic, and diplomatic failures in recent years have unfavorably affected our international image.

What many analysts fail to recognize, however, is that a large number of the principal overseas criticisms of the United States are not new, but even date back several decades or more. The present volume stands as living testimony to this fact, and the author hopes that it will dispel many misconceptions as to foreign attitudes towards America, especially the one that the world has turned against us overnight. The postscript in particular stresses this point, inasmuch as it specifically relates present criticisms of the United States to prior ones.

In the process of collecting material for use here approximately one thousand books were examined, as well as hundreds of magazine and journal articles, the great majority of them in English, but a considerable minority in French and German. Actually only a limited portion of this gigantic mass of printed material was deemed worthy of citation, since many of the works which were examined were little more than collages of naive descriptions, well-known facts, and hashed-over ideas. In the final reckoning, however, over a hundred tomes and several dozen periodical pieces were employed in this study. Nothing written before 1919 has been analyzed for the reason that the period between that date and 1960 constitutes a definite historical unit, as will be explained in the postscript.

Critics may be disturbed by the fact that the present volume concentrates on the European intelligentsia, since many of them consider what the European masses think to be a more important phenomenon. This is a mistaken belief for at least two reasons. In the first place, there is a great deal of similarity between the beliefs of the recluse in the ivory tower and the man in the street, and this is evidenced by a comparison of the material in the book proper with that in the post-script. Secondly, it is possible by means of an analysis of the writings of the elite to determine why they have reached certain conclusions about the United States, while this is much more difficult in the case of the opinions of the citizenry. Far too much attention has been paid in the past to how many people hold to an idea and far too little to how they arrive at it, and an attempt is made here to rectify this error.

Despite the fact that the works of seventy modern European authors are mentioned in these pages, certain ones are of much greater significance than others. As a result, the writings of Arnold Toynbee, Harold Laski, Denis Brogan, Andre Siegfried, Bernard Fay, Hermann von Keyserling, and M. J. Bonn are stressed. The material presented in this study is treated in terms of an overall synthesis rather than as a series of individual studies of various key figures, mainly for the reason that the latter expedient would focus attention on the analysts themselves rather than on European thought as a whole. This does not mean that the unique insights of these gifted thinkers are neglected; for these are emphasized along with the main currents in contemporary European opinion on the United States.

It is pointed out towards the end of this work that we frequently obtain a rather distorted picture as to what Europeans think of us, and it should be noted in conjunction with the above material that Europeans also visualize American life somewhat astigmatically at times. Admittedly the United States Information Agency and the Voice of America have done wonders in presenting the truth about us abroad, but they must overcome such obstacles as an inadequate dissemination of American journalism overseas, a tendency to justify ourselves through statistics, and a reliance on technique rather than content in spreading propaganda. It is doubtless true, as George Allen points out, that "ninety per cent of the impression which the United State makes abroad depends on our policies," but Allen also observes that the way that these are explained does affect our international standing to some extent. The scope of the present volume quite naturally precludes any lengthy study of the ways that Europeans inform themselves about America, yet this is an important consideration which one must constantly keep in mind when evaluating the material presented here.

Since there are certain aspects of this book which may puzzle the reader, an attempt will now be made to anticipate and answer some of the questions that he may pose after perusing it. While a large number of European commentators are cited here, it doubtless will be asked why such distinguished men of letters as George Macauley Treveylan, Albert Camus, and Benedetto Croce are absent from these pages. The reason for this is that their writings (at least those examined) are void or practically void of observations on the United States, not that they were deemed unworthy of inclusion. In addition, it will be perceived that there are only a handful of instances in this work in which a prominent European thinker is quoted in regard to one of his contemporaries, either to support his own position or to offer a rebuttal. Surprising as it may seem, most foreign writers fail to refer to other trans-Atlantic critics when they pen books and articles dealing with America, and thus such references are at a minimum here.

The effect of nationality on interpretation is another factor which is not stressed in this study, primarily for the reason that as a whole writers from one European country are no more hostile or friendly than are those from another. It is pointed out in the fourteenth chapter, however, that the relationship between America and the various nations of Europe does vary somewhat from country to country, and this is evidenced by the material presented in that chapter on England and France. Some critics may complain that not enough attention is devoted to the evolution of European thought on the United States in certain areas. But with the exception of diplomacy and culture there has been no marked change over the last forty years in trans-Atlantic attitudes towards this nation, at least up to the recent decline in American prestige. It must be remembered, moreover, that there has been a movement here away from isolationism towards internationalism, as well as one from cultural imitation towards cultural origination, so that a corresponding shift in European sentiment is only natural.

In closing, the author wishes to affirm in the strongest language possible that this book deals with the favorable as well as the unfavorable observations which European analysts of the United States have penned since 1919. Admittedly more emphasis is placed on criticisms in the introduction and the postscript; but this has been done for the reason that it has been the adverse judgments directed against the United States from overseas which have focused our attention on what others think of us. Such a stress, moreover, should in no way obscure the fact that over the past forty years laudations from across the Atlantic have far exceeded condemnations, so that the text proper places a greater emphasis on the more positive European evaluations of American life. But if it is a mistake to overestimate our weaknesses, it is also an error to overmagnify our strengths, and the present volume is offered with the object of placing the two in their proper perspective.

EDWARD CHESTER

Chapter I

UNITY VERSUS DIVERSITY

The presumption that there exist unique features by which one people or nation may be distinguished from another has its roots in the mists of antiquity. This theory often accompanies the belief that a nation has a special destiny to fulfill; in conjunction these ideas have bred an atmosphere more likely to be chauvinistic than peaceful. Such a sense of contrast is strikingly in evidence in the writings of those European intellectuals who have evaluated the role of America in the modern world. While the relationships they have discerned are not always ones of contrast between the Old World and the New, the differences they have detected are sufficiently numerous to establish a whole series of polarities with the United States and their continent at opposite extremes.

As the physical setting is the stage on which history takes place, it is only appropriate that this study should begin with an examination of European observations on the natural environment of this nation. An opinion representative of the belief that the United States and Europe differ physically is the remark made by the English biographer Hilaire Belloc that the "external world, that nature of soil and tree and landscape, in which the American soul has been formed, is as removed from the Old World as is one living species from another." This author's perception that the North American continent possesses a certain metallic quality may strike one as being overly picturesque. On the other hand, the extent to which foreign commentators have made equally fanciful characterizations of the United States may indicate that certain physical features are present here which are absent from Europe.

In contrast, the English political scientist Harold Laski, who is a bit less colorful than his colleague, views the difference as quantitative rather than qualitative. Laski observes that the very bigness of America "creates the belief that America is different, is somehow exceptional, that there is reserved for its citizens another destiny from that which is to befall the Old World." Such a point of view often characterizes the writings of those foreign thinkers who claim that an abundance of natural resources rather than an unequalled human ingenuity underlies American "superiority." By ascribing our "superiority" to this factor, they often cushion the psychological blow that the decline of Europe has dealt them, although this is not a totally satisfactory explanation.

One might surmise, therefore, that trans-Atlantic critics would regard the environment of the New World with envy and resentment, yet the fact is that quite a few observers even exhibit a certain reverence for the untamed, primeval state out of which the civilization of this nation has evolved. A belief that the natural forces around the American will continue to effect his development is reflected in the German philosopher Hermann von Keyserling's observation that "it may be expected of American nature that it can create the body which is a match for the constantly increasing mental tension, and which would be capable of perpetual change." On the other hand, many foreign analysts apparently feel that the balance between man and nature has been destroyed in the United States, and they regard this as one of the great tragedies of our time.

Von Keyserling, however, is not alone in his judgment that nature is still a potent force in the New World. Despite the increasing control of the environment in America via the machine, the French Dominican Raymond Bruckberger writes of this country as one in which "Nature is mistress in her own house," and the French existentialist author Simone de Beauvoir opines that it "remains one of the most unexplored in the world." In a slightly different vein, the French economist Andre Siegfried reminds us that conquest is not adaptation, a point so obvious it is often overlooked. Siegfried's remark that "time avenges itself for what is done outside of it" is hardly an expression of approval, as this implies that American civilization is out of step with nature and thus headed for eventual disaster.

The adaptation that the white settlers made to the environment of the New World differed, of course, quite drastically from that of the Indians. But whether the environment *per se* was sufficiently invigorating to produce a new civilization on this side of the Atlantic is rather questionable.

Taking for granted the assumption that no new civilization has arisen in America, the English historian Arnold Toynbee argues that the failure of the environment of the New World to stimulate the growth of one bolsters his contention that the environment of Western Europe was not responsible for the genesis of a new civilization in that area, either. (This, however, may be a *non sequitur*.) On the other hand, such a prominent thinker as the French historian Bernard

Fay in discussing the Anglo-Saxon and Spanish colonies emphasized the natural setting as the key element in the historical evolution of North America. Thus Fay writes of this country that "the special conditions offer to the human being an unheard of stimulus, train him in exaggerated expenditures of energy, and use him." This statement is somewhat at variance with the theory of Toynbee just mentioned, since it places more emphasis on the physical surroundings or environment as a factor of importance in the development of civilization here, and it is a matter of considerable dispute as to which analyst is the more correct in his diagnosis.

But if one defines the American environment in terms of sheer size, he will find wholesale agreement among European writers that space has been a significant element in the historical growth of the United States. To cite two typical examples, Andre Siegfried contends that Europe "is all articulation while America is all massivity," while Hilaire Belloc observes that "the great quality of the American rhythm is shortness of scale as applied to time and the opposite as applied to space, compared with the European rhythm." In continuing his comparison, Belloc remarks that "*space is less*" in the United States from both the horizontal and vertical points of view; he obviously believes that Americans think in larger spatial units than do Europeans. Also sensitive to the correlations made between America and space and Europe and time is the French historian Amaury de Riencourt, who comments that "the background of America, after all, is *space* and the Americans are sensitive above all to bigness, size, the lateral extension of immensity rather than depth." All three writers thus refer to a physical contrast between the United States and Europe, and those who make a comparison here decidedly reflect a minority viewpoint.

Continuing on this spatial theme, Raymond Bruckberger maintains that Americans are so intoxicated by the almost limitless expanses of space present in their country that they lack a sense of boundaries. Moreover, since space is so abundant here, it is not surprising that quite a few European writers speak of an American tendency to think and build geometrically. As the German psychologist Richard Muller-Freienfels sums up the situation, "the enormous distances of the continent are to be overcome only if the shortest connecting-line, the absolutely straight line, is followed by railroads and highways, though this course may be extremely expensive." Muller-Freienfels' further observation that any organic form (i.e., natural, non-geometric) would be both impractical and ridiculous in America does not, of course,

hold true in the case of the creations of such a genius as Frank
Lloyd Wright. It must be agreed, however, that in general "the
straight line and the stereometric mass" are the rule rather than the
exception in the United States. In addition, Simone de Beauvoir
maintains that this tendency may have unfortunate ramifications for
American life as a whole; she observes that Americans "want to run
their lives on geometrical rather than on wise lines; geometry is
learned, whereas wisdom is acquired." This perceptive statement
obviously refers to those Americans who desire to construct a perfect
world, and who then find out to their dismay that life is incapable
of being reduced to mathematical categories.

A few remarks about American cities, usually cited as a prime
example of the "geometrization" of life in the United States, are also
in order. In observing that the brick shanties vary in the same
manner as to height in Detroit as they do in Albuquerque or San
Antonio, the French existentialist philosopher Jean Paul Sartre throws
into focus the standardization which has accompanied this supposed
reduction of American life to geometrical terms. Raymond Bruckberger similarly speaks of "cities that can be indefinitely developed
by vermicular movements, endless additions of elements identical
with the preceding ones, like the growth of a sponge or a honeycomb."
Accordingly, it is not surprising that numerous observers, including
quite a few Americans, find the cities of this nation to be monoton-
ously similar despite local differences. This belief has led the editors
of *Fortune* to complain in their book *The Exploding Metropolis* of the
stereotyped and unimaginative development projects that now blight
the country with their boring similarity.

A reference was made earlier to the temporal factor which so many
writers stress when they contrast Europe and America. Europeans as
a whole have a considerable distaste for the American attitude towards
time, and this is strikingly revealed in their observations on American
cities. For example, that foe of American life, the French novelist
Georges Duhamel, acidly observes that America "erects, not monu-
ments, but merely buildings." Jean-Paul Sartre more cooly reflects
that "we Europeans change within changeless cities, and our houses
and neighborhoods outlive us; American cities change faster than
their inhabitants do, and it is the inhabitants who outlive the cities."
Similarly, in comparing the life expectancy of dwelling houses and
factories in America to that of a dog, the English novelist Wyndham
Lewis writes of the short life span and feverish vitality so characteristic of both.[1] Raymond Bruckberger also opines, in obvious reference

to the supposed non-permanence of buildings in the United States, that "our grandnephews will know the America of our time only through photographs." Taken as a whole, these remarks constitute a ringing condemnation of the transitoriness of American life, and thus may be taken in conjunction with the charge that America is lacking in historical tradition.

A slightly different twist to these observations is given by Arnold Toynbee, who comments that "it is only on second thoughts that it occurs to him (the European observer) that, in all but one or two of the European cities that are to-day in the full swim of modern Western life, nine-tenths of the buildings are no older than ten-tenths of those in Buffalo or Pittsburgh." As this statement was made in 1939, Toynbee did not have the opportunity to include in his estimate the devastation of European cities that took place during World War II. Thus the percentage of dwellings of ancient vintage standing in that part of the world today is even less. On the other hand, it must be admitted that European critics are generally correct in their claim that American buildings are temporary rather than permanent; many examples could be cited which prove this point.

Returning to the spatial theme again, quite a few European observers are of the opinion that the natural landscape of this country, despite its immense size, is characterized by the same uniformity as American cities. Thus after surveying the broad expanses of this nation, the Austrian economist M. J. Bonn comments that "America's mantle is more of one tint . . . rain and sunshine, frost and the glow of summer have toned down the somewhat glaring uniformity into innumerable shades of color. But they can only modify and not extinguish the great degree of uniformity which still remains, woven by nature and colored by man." Since there are both natural and man-made types of standardization present in this country, one would expect that the civilization that has evolved here would likewise be uniform in nature. Such is not the case, however, as it is generally recognized that pronounced differences do exist between Massachusetts and Louisiana or California and Ohio, for example, as well as between larger subdivisions of this country.

These dissimilarities, moreover, once inspired Frederick Jackson Turner to publish a work entitled *The Significance of Sections in American History*. In this collection of essays Turner set forth the thesis that the United States was a federation of sections and that disputes and even wars have resulted because of the varied and sometimes rival interests of these sections. The stress he places on sectionalism is also somewhat typical of the writings of many other American historians, and has apparently influenced European thought to a considerable degree.[2] Although the term "regionalism" is on occasion used in its place, this expression does not imply as sharp a cleavage between the various parts of the nation as sectionalism does. As a result, the North, the West, and the South will be considered as sections rather than as regions in the following pages.

While most Europeans talk in general terms of the South and the West, New York City is to many of them the personification of the North, and as such has become a focal point in their writings. There are few if any journals or diaries which omit references to this metropolis. While only a handful of European writers fail to express their admiration for New York City, the enthusiasm of those that do is usually of a rather cold variety. Jean-Paul Sartre, for example, describes America's largest city as an "immense and malevolent space" in which "all the hostility and cruelty of Nature are present." The French liberal Odette Keun similarly refers to it as an embodiment of man's fancies that "grew and swelled so promptly and monstrously that now it has become inhuman." On a broader plane, Richard Muller-Freienfels reflects a criticism that has been levelled against the United States as a whole when he characterizes the city front in terms of "quantity rather than quality" and of "conspicuous uniformity." The point of view expressed by Simone de Beauvoir that "New York is not America" does not appear to be representative of the majority opinion abroad that this city in many ways is typical of American life.

Indeed, this rather cold reception of New York is mirrored in numerous observations made about the North as a whole. To Hermann von Keyserling, speed in the North "is not an expression of strength, but merely of neurotic restlessness" and "it is certain as a mathematical truth that the Northerner's world philosophy will not stand the pragmatic test for any length of time." These remarks should be taken in conjunction with von Keyserling's belief that a rather slow, unhurried pace of life is necessary for the fullest development of a civilization. Even less complimentary is Arnold Toynbee, who speaks of the decline of artistic creativity in New England, using the deserted village of Town Hill, Connecticut as evidence that human enterprise now has moved on towards the Pacific. Toynbee observes that "in this hard environment of New England, an apprenticeship had been served for the hard task of building the United States. When the apprentice had felt himself fully trained in nerve and muscle and skill, he had simply left the place which had been his training-ground and had gone to the place where he was to do his work in life." It should be noted here, however, that von Keyserling has a special bias for the South and Toynbee for the West, and these prejudices should be kept in mind while one is evaluating these comments.

If one were required to explain this slightly acid attitude of certain European observers towards the North and especially New York, he might suggest that to Europeans the North lacks such redeeming features as the frontier spirit of the West or the cultured leisure of the Old South, but instead symbolizes the materialist money-making ideal at its very worst. In addition, the North has been historically that part of the country through which European culture and customs permeated America. Thus by criticizing the North, overseas observers may be expressing their displeasure at those undesirable aspects of their own way of life which they see reflected in this nation. It is, in fact, even conceivable that Europeans feel that those American writers who flaunt the alleged superiority of America over Europe are usually Northerners, and that this factor effects in an adverse manner their judgments on this section.

But whatever their emotional reaction is to it, it is perhaps surprising that the North has not stimulated more original thinking from European critics than they have manifested in their writings. The observations that they do make are invariably stereotyped, as the advantage of detachment that they possess has not resulted in ideas any more striking than those offered by their American counterparts. Admittedly both New York City and New England have been extensively analyzed by American writers, and thus the argument might be set forth that there is little unique left to say. The same thing, however, is true of the West and the South, but this has not dammed the flow of provocative remarks from the pens of Europeans in regard to them. One might offer the obvious explanation that Northerners are more similar to Europeans than are Southerners and Westerners, so that as a result Europeans are not as able to discern the original features in Northern life. On the other hand, the general tendency of Europeans to reject the North (and especially New York) may warrant the conclusion that they believe that unique characteristics of an undesirable nature are present in the latter section, and they do not want these also to be attributed to Europe.

The West differs from the North in that it seems to be the center of European admiration for the United States. The English writer Rom

Landau, for example, expresses the sentiment that "as I moved West-ward, I found greater sincerity, modesty and open-mindedness; a more genuine desire to learn and to broaden the mental horizon; a less intense preoccupation with immediate results." While such factors as population pressure and the various Indian wars are often cited in analyzing the role of the West in American history, the most im-portant force has been, of course, the frontier. Raymond Bruckberger sums up the significance of this phenomenon most admirably in his remark that the frontier "does not in the least evoke the idea of a natural or legal boundary, but rather a vacuum, a vague terrain, a summons from the open air, and the corresponding movement to fill the vacuum, occupy the terrain, reply to the summons." It would be possible to elaborate on these three factors at length, but since their importance is almost universally recognized abroad, it seems desirable to pass on to more controversial interpretations of the West offered by European critics.

Quite a few of these interpretations are as "wild" as the legend about that part of the nation which they purportedly analyze. There are many American scholars, for example, who would take issue with the French journalist Andre Tardieu's blunt assertion that "it was the West that furnished the melting-pot for immigration." The geo-graphical factor obviously was not the decisive one here, for the big cities of America were the main centers of fusion. Similarly, Tardieu's equation of the maturation of the West with the emergence of the United States as a world power does not necessarily prove a causal relationship, but rather reflects a chronological proximity between the closing of the frontier (1890) and the Venezuelan boundary dispute of 1895, or the Spanish-American War of 1898. But even more provoking is Amaury de Riencourt's opinion that "it is clear that civilization was going to rise in the West without going through the intermediate stage of Culture." This remark does little to explain how the non-European features of the West manifested themselves, and even more important, omits a description of the stage of growth supposedly passed over.

Perhaps a bit more in line with traditional assessments of the West is M. J. Bonn's observation that "the West gave the people of the United States fairly equal opportunities; it made it possible for them to evolve a competitive capitalistic society." One might also cite as valid the English historian Frank Thistlethwaite's remark that "the individualism natural to the West . . . gave form and purpose to self-improvement." In addition, most critics would accept the statement of Bertrand Russell that the civilization of the West was "more self-conscious (than its Northern and Southern counterparts), without sufficient roots in tradition, rather machine-made, and unduly utilitarian." Although these concepts are less original than the observations mentioned in the preceding paragraph, they are also more factually accurate and less open to question.

The theories of Arnold Toynbee concerning the West are likewise significant in that they present a stimulating approach to this section which does not do violence to the facts. Toynbee believes, for example, that the short-lived Cattle Kingdom (A.D. 1866 to A.D. 1877) furnishes a means of reconstructing by analogy the birth of the pastoral civilization on the Eurasian Steppe two or three millenia before the birth of Christ. By comparing the cowboys of the New World with the nomads of the old, Toynbee is able to present added insights into the post-Civil War era in the West. As they explain historical phenomena on a world-wide rather than a sectional basis, such imaginative observations serve as a correction both to those who maintain that the events of the West were unique and to those who support the opposing point of view, and accordingly should be used as the basis for further studies.

The South presents a more complex phenomenon than does the West in that it is variously regarded as a past, a present, and a future by observers abroad. Yet regardless of what it once was or what it may eventually become, this section is now stereotyped as something of an ugly duckling. As the English political scientist Denis Brogan pessimistically comments, "the South is analogous to the poor, feud-ridden, historically unfortunate border countries between Germany and Russia." Odette Keun similarly writes of "the waste of its resources, the erosion of its soil, the beastly poverty of its rural slums, its dreadful housing, its starvation wages, (and) its terrible diseases." Less kind here than in dealing with the West, Arnold Toynbee maintains that the poor whites in the Old South (along with those in the Union of South Africa) are "the most flagrant examples of 'proletarianization' in a post-Modern Western World." With such a bad press, it is not surprising that the Communists have seized this section of the country as a typical example of American decadence and have indoctrinated their subjects with the novels of William Faulkner and Erskine Caldwell.

Few will deny that the environment has been a factor of considerable importance in the historical development of the South. For example, the English historian James Bryce claims that the climate

has been more of a retarding influence here than in the North and
the French novelist Andre Maurois similarly maintains that "the
tempo is more slow than in the rest of America." But whether this
relatively slow rate of life has been accompanied by a superior civilization is open to question. While a person of Harold Laski's intellectual temperament maintains that "the legend of Southern culture
is, in a high degree, nothing more than another example of that
fertile confusion between leisure and culture," a Hermann von Keyserling finds that Virginia is the only region of the United States "which
has a general cultural atmosphere in a wide sense." These two
diverse views, however, may be reconciled on the basis that they
reflect differing views on what constitutes a civilization.

That the pre-Civil War South was in many ways at loggerheads
with the rest of the nation is readily admitted both here and abroad.
In differentiating the South from the North, Frank Thistlethwaite
perceptively observes that the Southerner of that day subjugated his
individualism to the accepted social ethic and looked to seventeenth
century England, medieval Christendom, and ancient Greece for
his ideal rather than to the future. But any attempt today to evaluate
in an objective manner the achievements of the South of that era is
difficult because of the generally democratic bias prevalent among
thinkers. Accordingly, the English philosopher Bertrand Russell
speaks of Southern politicians of the mid-Nineteenth Century in
terms of imperialism and oligarchy, obviously implying that the
presence of these two elements condemns a society. Even if one
expresses his admiration for nineteenth century Southern culture,
he must pay homage to the belief that the ends do not justify the
means, and grudgingly admit that this civilization was bought at too
high a cost.

While critics of modern Southern life attack that section on
numerous counts, those European writers of today who speak of a
resurgent South usually do so in terms of industrial growth. Whether
or not one dates this growth from 1919, as does Andre Siegfried, or
from 1939, as does the Swedish sociologist Gunnar Myrdal, the fact
remains evident that the South is presently on the march. In addition, if one is to believe Hermann von Keyserling, the future holds
even brighter prospects in store for the South. As von Keyserling
writes, "once quality has been recognized as the decisive factor, this
will in its turn lead to the predominance of the superior human type.
And such a superior native type is to be found only in the South today." Few if any European writers claim that the Negro problem in

that section has been solved, but this in no way invalidates the progress that has been made in other spheres of the South.

Focusing on the national scene again, it seems to be the consensus abroad that a movement away from sectionalism in the United States is now in effect. Representative of this point of view is the English biographer Philip Guedalla's observation that along with a tendency towards economic interdependence, "the swift growth of modern transportation (has) made a unit of their (America's) vast and scattered territories." M. J. Bonn likewise supports this belief in his assertion that there exists in America a trend toward unification. Bonn expresses a minority view, moreover, when he predicts that "a strong growth of national regionalism, much as it existed in the thirteen original states a hundred and fifty years ago" will soon ensue, as most writers stress its continued decline. It is indeed conceivable that the ultimate outcome of this battle between unity and diversity in American life may hinge on some unknown factor, but few would question that considerable progress has been made towards consolidation.

In conclusion, it might be noted that one of the most baffling aspects of modern European thought on America is that foreigners so glibly employ the term "American" to describe the typical inhabitant of this nation. If this word is to be used in a valid manner, the differences between the inhabitants of the various parts of the United States must be relatively limited. Many European analysts, however, strongly emphasize the dissimilarities between the citizenry of the various sections, yet refer to the "American" rather than to the "Northerner" or the "Westerner" or the "Southerner" when making generalizations about this country. Of course, it is just as illogical for an American to write of the "European" after citing the differences between the English, the French, the Germans, and the Italians, although one error does not justify another. But human thought is at times a strange process, and such *non sequiturs* must be tolerated with patience.

CHAPTER II

THE MELTING POT AT WORK

It is generally agreed that no nation is entirely unified racially; America is obviously no exception to this rule. Many individuals, however, view with mixed feelings the recent changes in a country which once appeared to be racially unified except for Negroes and Indians. To one group it is a tribute to the willingness of America to open its gates to the needy of the world in the past, but to another it is a proof of an undesirable modification of national character. Up to the end of World War I, unlimited immigration into America was more or less encouraged by the government, but the original "Anglo-Saxon" stock was diluted as the percentage of newcomers arriving from Southeastern Europe increased. Congress placed a series of restrictions on further immigration into the United States during the 1920's as a result of protests against this "watering", so that racial modifications in the America of today should be attributed more to intermarriage than to the addition of new racial stocks.

That this now diminished stream of immigrants has been of spiritual importance to America is widely recognized. The French philosopher Jacques Maritain, for example, writes that "it is to be hoped that that strange source of insuperable strength and energy which comes from the influx of the poor and the humiliated, welcomed here to live a worthy human life, will never cease to vitalize American civilization." The importance of immigration in American history is also noted by Frank Thistlethwaite, who observes that to a considerable degree the American national character has been the result of migration, while the British as a rule has not. (This statement ignores the importance of immigration right down to the present in English history.) Both remarks, of course, strongly stress that America was not born fully developed in 1776 or 1789, but has been in the process of constant expansion since that date. These observations also emphasize the fact that this growth has not been a strictly organic process in which no outside factor was present, but mutative and irregular in nature, since it has been greatly influenced by such alien forces as immigration.

In observing that the first protective tariffs were enacted by Congress partly as a result of an "intensive immigration", the French journalist Lucien Romier declares that "a choice had to be made between men and merchandise, in view of the danger of having too many men and being unable to feed them and keep them busy."[3] Most authorities, however, feel that the imposition of a high set of duties on imports was primarily due to the need of protecting infant industries, and thus Romier's thesis does not appear to be substantiated historically despite its tantalizing logic. Another interesting theory is set forth by Bertrand Russell, who correlates free land and immigrant labor as factors in the historical development of America. Russell also maintains that the reduction of surplus land to a minimum after 1890 was shortly followed by a strict restriction on immigration. This idea is more plausible than Romier's, but errs in its reference to "cheap" labor, regardless of the fact that the immigrant was paid less than the native-born American. Actually labor in the United States has generally been confronted with a "demand" market, and thus has been the beneficiary of a far higher standard of living than that enjoyed by European workers.

More in line with the facts are the views of Arnold Toynbee, who writes that during the Nineteenth Century "an American family's rise in the social scale had thus been almost automatic at every level in the structure of a social pyramid that was being jacked up and underpinned by the importation of a fresh layer of immigrant population year by year." It is strange that so obvious an insight has escaped the attention of those Americans who opposed immigration on the grounds that the flood of newcomers would lower the general level of society. In also stressing that the immigrants would furnish an integral market for the "increasing abundance of commodities" produced here, Toynbee explains in a more convincing manner than does Romier why the United States did not adhere to free trade during the latter part of the Nineteenth Century. As Toynbee implies, an expansion in production must be followed by a corresponding increase in consumption, either internal or external, or economic disaster must necessarily ensue.

In regard to the more recent period of American history, many Europeans have condemned the United States severely for imposing restrictions on immigration. Critics abroad have often claimed that these restrictions were the result of the slanderous assumption that Southeastern Europeans (who by the turn of the century made up the bulk of the immigrants) were "inferior." Andre Siegfried even goes so far as to state that a hostility towards foreigners was the main feature of "Normalcy," and the French writer Lucien Lehman

observes of the immigration laws of the 1920's that "no argument can
be logically advanced in their favor." Elsewhere Siegfried refers to the
Malthusian theory (population increases faster than the means of
subsistence), as he maintains that the American government placed
bans on further immigration because of Malthusian considerations.
He thus implies that there existed a widespread feeling in this country
at the time that its powers of economic expansion were limited. This
attitude certainly has not been noticeably evident in the United
States, except perhaps during the depths of a depression.

European criticisms of American immigration policy generally
range over a much wider expanse of territory than the limited plots
staked out by the above authors. Arnold Toynbee, for example,
writes that restrictive legislation had the effect of producing in the
United States "a penalized and alienated class" which "might perhaps one day find the makings of a 'fifth column.'" Although insufficient time has passed for a full assessment of the validity of Toynbee's thesis, there does not exist at the moment much historical evidence to support his position. On the other hand, M. J. Bonn
strikes at a more sensitive point in his accusation that America "no
longer will be the eulogized land for the economically, politically, and
socially oppressed masses of Europe." [4] It is indeed true that the down-
trodden European proletariat is no longer able to flee its homeland for
the more inviting shores of this country. But many Americans claim
that Bonn's belief reflects a sour grapes attitude in that Europe is
now forced to care for what it once dumped abroad, and their reasoning does have a certain validity.

Other European thinkers do not censure the immigration policies
of this nation to such an exaggerated extent. Thus Gunnar Myrdal
admits that America was not the only country to oppose unlimited
immigration in the post-World War I period, although Myrdal does
state that the American restrictions were "certainly among the
extreme." Bernard Fay actually expresses gratitude that these limitations were imposed, as he is of the opinion that the further loss
of population via emigration would have an adverse effect on the
French economy. Even such a critic of American immigration policy
as Andre Siegfried may be aligned by implication on the side of restrictions. After referring to such choice fruits of local culture as the
intellectual achievements of New England and the French cookery
of Louisiana, he sadly comments that "the factor that made this
America unrecognizable in that which was to follow it was the third
wave of immigration that de-Anglicized the country." Obviously, a

limitation on further *arrivees* was the only way to halt the trend, although Siegfried does not draw that conclusion in this passage.

Inasmuch as a close connection exists between the two, it is only logical that an analysis of the extent of racial prejudice here should follow an examination of American immigration policies. There is a widespread belief abroad that racism exists in the United States; Raymond Bruckberger strongly affirms that in "the racist experiment, purely negative and stained with sin . . . lies the greatest danger to America as a nation. Many of us, moreover, hold similar views.

Jacques Maritain, another French Catholic, opines in rebuttal that "nothing resembling a racist doctrine exists in America," although he admits that prejudice does exist in this country to a certain degree. Gunnar Myrdal, whose remarks tend to support Maritain's position, refers to "the gradual destruction (here) of the popular theory behind race prejudice," and it would seem that it would be impossible for racism to survive without a certain amount of theoretical underpinning. The crucial question is, therefore, not whether certain racial or ethnical groups are discriminated against in the United States, but whether these unfair practices are strongly rooted in an underlying philosophy of white, and more particularly, Anglo-Saxon supremacy. Some sort of determination of the extent to which there is a correlation between practice and theory in American racial discrimination is thus necessary.

Actually the outstanding exponents of Anglo-Saxon supremacy have been Europeans, as Houston Stewart Chamberlain and Count de Gobineau rank far higher as theorists of this doctrine than do such Americans as John W. Burgess and Josiah Strong. In addition, there has never arisen a Hitler in the United States to carry through this doctrine to its logical conclusion, although this was the unfortunate fate of Europe only a few short years ago. It is true that in the Old South (and to a lesser extent in the South of today) racial discrimination had a theoretical base, but here this discrimination was focused less on white supremacy than on the Negro's status as a slave and on his supposed mental and moral inferiority. This is a distinction that many European commentators fail to make, and even more significant is the fact that in many respects the role of the Anglo-Saxon in American life is taken for granted rather than consciously singled out for special emphasis.

The English writer Norman Angell thus points out that an "English vote" has never existed in America, despite the fact that for a long period of time the English component of the immigrant amalgam was the most important one. In contrast, the Italians, to cite a prominent example, have often in the past voted so nearly as a unit that politicians of both parties have maneuvered to snare their votes. The English historian Lewis Namier likewise observes that it is considered bad taste for Anglo-Saxons in the United States to show any feeling for their native land (England), although many of the other minority groups of America often flaunt their origins by means of national festival days and similar devices. M. J. Bonn casts further light on this subject by his statement that early in the history of this country "Anglicization" and "Americanization" were almost synonymous. According to Bonn, an American who boasted of his English ancestry after the American Revolution was bitterly criticized by other Americans, since the latter naturally desired to stress the differences rather than the similarities between the newly independent United States and England. As a result, individuals with an Anglo-Saxon background often hesitate to emphasize their racial heritage even today, and this generally has been a deterrent to the development of a philosophy of Anglo-Saxon supremacy in America.

Here an examination of the Negro is in order, both because he is the focal point of the white supremacy controversy, and because he is a representative minority group. Obviously the Negro differs from the white man; more often than not this difference is interpreted as a token of inferiority by his detractors. The belief that a person or group is different, however, is quite often a sign of superiority, and an examination of the Negro and his way of life brings to light many qualities useful to the development of an advanced civilization. It is quite striking that European thinkers of the caliber of Wyndham Lewis and Hermann von Keyserling have evaluated the Negro as a positive rather than as a negative social force; it is to them that we turn for a presentation of the case for the Negro.

In a statement that has few parallels for bluntness, Wyndham Lewis flatly asserts that "American civilization as we know it owes more, probably, to the Negro than to anybody." To Lewis the Negroes are the "artistic leaven" of the United States. This observation must be interpreted in terms of general Negro influences on such cultural phenomena as jazz and neo-primitive art, rather than in terms of the contributions to American civilization of particular Negro literary, musical or artistic geniuses. Lewis also attributes to the Negro such personality traits as warm-heartedness and mirthfulness; he believes that these characteristics have had a great influence on American society. But here even more than in the prior instance the impact of the Negro on the life of this nation has been a racial rather than an individual one. As one of Lewis' favorite theories is that a new way of life is developing in this country, he obviously thinks that the Negro is going to play an important role in the process.

Hermann von Keyserling, who is also convinced of the cultural importance of the American Negro, ventures the opinion that "the coloured man alone of all settlers surrendered himself immediately to the spirit of the New Earth," and that as a result he "was able to develop an authentic soul." Von Keyserling here obviously equates the soul with emotional life; divining that a void exists in the subconsciousness of the white American, he observes that the Negro has moved in to fill this gap. This reasoning would be more convincing were it not for the fact that there also is an element among the whites characterized by an emotional rather than intellectual attitude toward life (the backwoodsmen of Appalachia, for instance). It must be admitted, moreover, that this component has contributed little or nothing to the development of a higher civilization in the United States. Here, as is often the case, von Keyserling exhibits his strong prejudice against over-intellectualization, but in the process he at time lapses into praise of the equally undesirable trait of over-emotionalizing.

On the other hand, Arnold Toynbee seems to be somewhat disenchanted with the cultural role that the Negro has played in the development of this country. Toynbee speaks, for example, of "the American Negro debasement of the Western Christian religious coinage." He does observe elsewhere, however, that the Negro has rediscovered in Christianity "certain original meanings and values which Western Christendom has long ignored." The author of *A Study of History* also refers to "the triumph of a Negro art in the northern states of America" as a "signal victory for Barbarism," and he makes particular reference to the importation of West African music and sculpture. Toynbee, of course, often stresses that the introduction of primitive elements into an advanced civilization is a sign of decadence rather than revitalization. This point, moreover, must be kept in mind while one is evaluating his observations on the Negro, whom he regards as occupying a low position on the scale of cultural development.

Regardless of his achievements, the treatment that the Negro has suffered at the hands of his white brethren in the United States has provoked much comment abroad. Gunnar Myrdal echoes a widespread feeling in his assertion that "treatment of the Negro is Ameri-

ca's greatest and most conspicuous scandal." Since there is no real
Negro problem in contemporary Europe, Europeans are free to criticize
the racial situation in America without being charged with hypocrisy.
Thus the English and French are always eager to proclaim that
slavery was eliminated in the most remote parts of their far-flung
empires (in 1833 and 1848, respectively) prior to the abolition of
human bondage in the United States proper. Moreover, Arnold
Toynbee and other European writers often point out that Negroes are
treated more as equals in Europe than in America when they are confronted by the American claim that democracy has reached the peak
of its development in this country. As for the international ramifications of this dilemma, Gunnar Myrdal suggests that the treatment of
the Negro in the United States "is salt in their wounds" to the colored
people of the world. Now that the whites are in danger of losing their
ascendancy on the global scene, it is, of course, somewhat tactless for
Americans to goad the black and yellow races of the world into further
hostility by discriminating against the Negro here.

Most criticisms of the handling of the Negro question in the United
States are directed against the South; in this connection Europeans
are often rather vehement. Thus Arnold Toynbee points out the
ethical dishonesty involved in allowing Negroes in the South to wait on
whites in restaurants but not to eat with them. The Swiss theologian
Denis de Rougemont similarly observes that "who will dare say that
the problem has been completely solved, when liberals and Christians
still find the customs of the South a matter of complaint." Since the
Supreme Court decisions of 1954 trans-Atlantic castigators have
become even more critical than before.

As might be expected, European commentators do not regard the
life of the Negro in the North as ideal. Lucien Lehman, for
example, declares that above the Mason-Dixon Line "one is forced to
proclaim openly, according to the noble tradition, that the black man
is the equal of the white, but at the same time one strives to avoid his
presence in as far as possible." Gunnar Myrdal similarly observes that
although the Negro may have obtained in the North "practically una-
bridged civic equality . . . he is discriminated against ruthlessly in private relations." As a result, many Europeans maintain that the
unfair actions practiced against the Negro in the North are more
hypocritical than are those of the Southern variety; this criticism is
admittedly justified.

Quite a few writers already have noted that in recent years the
position of the American Negro has improved, at least economically,

although as a whole it is still inferior to that of the white man. Raymond Bruckburger states that a greater number of economic opportunities have been opened up to the Negro as the result of industrialization, but Gunnar Myrdal protests that the decreasing demand for unskilled labor as a result of technological advances has adversely affected his position. Denis Brogan likewise points out that the Congress of Industrial Organizations achieved a fine record in regard to the employment of Negroes, but that the score sheet of the American Federation of Labor in the past has been much less praiseworthy. (One should note that prior to their amalgamation the A. F. of L. had more skilled laborers than the C. I. O.) Admittedly such views are somewhat conflicting, but there is more agreement among overseas critics in the economic area than in the social one that the black man is slowly but surely advancing towards approximate equality with the white man in the United States.

This examination of viewpoints about the Negro leads into the final topic to be discussed here: the extent to which various minority and immigrant groups have been assimilated into American society. Opinions differ greatly as to how far this integration has gone, if indeed it has occurred at all. One of the more extreme statements denying that assimilation has taken place is that of Lucien Romier, who asserts that "one might go so far as to say that at the welcome hearth of this new home the attributes of each race become more sharply defined as if stripped of all useless features." Even if most European commentators deny that total assimilation has taken place, they reject Romier's thesis; in fact, the overwhelming majority claim that differences have decreased markedly as a result of immigration.

A less extreme representative of the anti-assimilation position is Philip Guedalla, who expresses the view that "the fabled melting-pot is not yet heated to a point at which the elements consent to fuse." Unfortunately Guedalla does not furnish the reader with any indication of the amount of extra heat needed to fuse the pot or how this heat is to be obtained. As of the early 1920's the eminent James Bryce also doubted that racial assimilation had taken place in the United States but he, unlike Guedalla, blamed the situation on insufficient time rather than on a lack of an adequate amount of social heat.[5] One might cite other barriers against fusion as well, especially cultural and (to a lesser degree) linguistic differences, since with the exception of the Negro these are as important, if not more so, than physical dissimilarities.

Those European critics who believe that the immigrant has been assimilated into the body social of this country are, as has just been pointed out, quite numerous. One might cite in this connection the rather paradoxical observation of the Spanish writer Salvador de Madariaga that "America's vast population is homogeneous, though composed for the most part of mongrels." Significantly, the opinion that such a condition as partial assimilation does not exist is quite widespread abroad. Thus the English historian J. A. Spender states that there are no half-way houses in which the immigrant may be gradually acclimatised, while the English essayist G. K. Chesterton similarly observes of New York City that the immigrant is either an exile or a citizen, but never a cosmopolitan.

There are some European writers who adopt the more subtle approach of Andre Siegfried that "in the American Melting Pot, the temperature at which fusion takes place varies with the different races." It is, however, quite difficult to present graphically the respective points on the scale at which the various groups of foreigners cease to be foreigners and become Americans. In any event one finds it exceedingly more difficult to prove that assimilation has taken place in the United States than to disprove it. This is because any evidence that foreign customs or traits still exist in America may be used to support the theory that assimilation has not occurred. But to bolster the opposing view it is necessary to demonstrate that these foreign customs or traits are absent—which they are not.

In summarizing the findings of this chapter, it should be stressed again that Europeans are well aware that the impact of the immigrant on American civilization has been considerable, and that this impact is still in evidence today. Since fewer immigrants have entered this nation in recent years, there is not much question that total assimilation will become a reality in the next century or two, if it has not yet taken place, as a minority of European critics claim. But the fact that the racial and ethnical differences of today will be less prominent in the future does not in any way decrease the importance of the Americanization of minority groups. It must be remembered that with the exception of the Negro social integration has been achieved in this nation by natural means rather than by governmental edict. Moreover, this process of natural integration is a significant feature of the democratic process at work, as it reveals both its positive features and in the case of the Negro, its shortcomings. For this reason, the whole subject is of as much interest to the political scientist as it is to the anthropologist.

Chapter III

THE AMERICAN CHARACTER

To the remainder of the world the United States is not only the symbol of a particular civilization or way of life, but also of a distinct mass personality. The object of this chapter is to examine some of the traits which European observers have assigned to that fictitious entity, the American character It may seem strange that such seemingly irreconcilable qualities as youthfulness and maturity, individualism and standardization, and tolerance and bigotry would be regarded abroad as being American characteristics. Still such opposite qualities as love and hate are often found simultaneously in the normal human personality, so that it is not inconceivable that other dissimilar combinations would occur also in the mass soul of a country. Of course, most commentators both here and abroad recognize that the American character is quite complex. Thus J. A. Spender notes that "the difficulty, when one turns it over in one's mind, is to harmonise so many apparently conflicting qualities," and American analysts often have observed the same thing.

Of all the aspects of the American character, it is perhaps the relative ascendancy of conformity over individualism that has caused the most concern among the European intelligentsia. One rarely encounters any similar quality mentioned by European critics in the place of individualism, but conformity often appears in the guise of standardization or uniformity. Admittedly conformity is essentially a social concept, while standardization and uniformity refer respectively to the impact of mass production and natural homogeneity on the United States, but an obvious relationship exists between all three terms. This linkage will be analyzed forthwith in an examination of the anti-individualistic element in American life.

All three of these traits (conformity, standardization, and uniformity) are usually looked upon with a critical eye by Europeans, but it is perhaps the first which is the most unpalatable to them. Thus Bertrand Russell writes of the "tyranny of the herd," observing that in the United States "eccentricity is frowned upon, and unusual opinions bring social penalties upon those who hold them."⁹ It is difficult to ascertain from just what roots this American tendency to conform sprang, but M. J. Bonn suggests that it is attributable to the influence of the pioneer, who "required that everyone should be like himself." It might be added here that the other key figure in the development of the United States, the Puritan, also expected others to be as he was. The fact that both the Puritan and the pioneer were suspicious of those who did not think or act as they did has, of course, led many European commentators to claim that the Americans are an intolerant people, which point will be discussed more fully later in this chapter.

In regard to the effect of standardization on this country, Lucien Romier observes that "innovations are not spread gradually from above down to the lower ranks," since "they assail the whole massed society at one stroke." Jean-Paul Sartre similarly contends in his essay "Individualism and Conformism in the United States" that the machine "acts as a universalizing factor" here. As Andre Maurois points out, this American tendency towards standardization may also be traced to the impact of science on our society. The impact, in connection with the influence of mass production, creates an atmosphere where that which is different is rejected as being imperfect, since it is difficult to fit it into the normal scheme of things. But despite this tendency towards standardization, Hermann von Keyserling and various other analysts abroad do admit that there is some variety in American life,[7] so that it is a fallacy to maintain that standardization is universally regarded as the invariable rule here.

Many European thinkers have noted that the American landscape has a monotonous quality because of its uniform nature, and they also have observed that the American people themselves are characterized by a similar uniformity. Thus George Duhamel affirms that "what strikes the European traveller is the progressive approximation of human life to what we know of the way of life of insects." Duhamel also suggests that the society which Maurice Maeterlinck describes in his classic *The Life of the Bee* has a parallel in the way of life now evolving in America. One may ignore Duhamel's observation as the ranting of an extremist, but it is less easy to explain away Andre Siegfried's observation that all Americans are astonishingly alike despite the diverse racial and ethnical make-up of the population. As for the social adhesion which is so characteristic of the United States, Hilaire Belloc offers a most plausible theory in his suggestion that the intense and repeated contacts of the American people with each other engenders uniformity. This is an obvious point which quite a few European commentators have failed to take note of; they often assign this phenomenon to more grandiose and elaborate causes.

There is perhaps only a minority of European critics who affirm that individualism is more characteristic of American life than conformity. Nevertheless, their ideas merit examination, especially because of the ingenious logic which they often use to support their position. Thus Lucien Romier offers the suggestion that "individualism does not show itself, as with the Latin people, by dissent from the general practice, on the part of the individual,—a negative individualism,—but on the contrary by the cultivation, the encouragement of those qualities in individuals which would offer the greatest advantage, the best chances for all." It is certainly true that to label a person an individualist because he is completely different is to misclassify a human caricature who may have few if any really positive qualities, but many persons define individualism in this manner.

Along somewhat different lines, Jean-Paul Sartre observes that the individual asserts his individualism within the conformist society of America by joining various clubs or assocations in which he is able to function as his true self. There is, however, a strong tendency to conform even within these private groups, so that Sartre's remark needs to be qualified. On the other hand, M. J. Bonn asserts that American individualism is "an individualism of normalcy, an individualism of the masses." Bonn's remark again demonstrates that those European thinkers who believe that individualism exists in this country usually have to give their thinking a quite unusual twist to make their point, and this twist is often so violent as to invalidate their observations.

Even those foreign commentators who do detect an individualistic element in American life frequently maintain that its influence is on the wane. As Amaury de Riencourt notes, "true individualism and originality, already weak in Tocqueville's America, was sinking under the weight of a psychological socialization exceeding anything known in the past." De Riencourt declares that World War I was an important milestone in the decline of individualism here, while Rom Landau asserts that this global conflict was the dividing line between the essentially individualist and the primarily conformist America. It might also be noted that such features hostile to individualism as the closing of the West and the widespread implementation of mass production were beginning to exert their full influence on American life at about this time. For these reasons and others, as Andre Siegfried points out, "the epoch of the pioneer has been replaced by the epoch of the machine." It, moreover, will be demonstrated in the seventh chapter that many European observers believe that an essential similarity exists between this nation and the Soviet Union in that mass life predominates in both at the expense of individuality.

Another highly controversial subject which merits examination here is whether this nation is youthful or mature. It is quite striking that quite a few European commentators (M. J. Bonn and the Spanish philosopher Jose Ortega y Gasset, for example) believe that the United States is younger than Europe. Moreover, Ortega y Gasset even claims that America "is a primitive people camouflaged behind the latest inventions." Lucien Romier and Andre Maurois also hold views similar to those of Bonn and Ortega y Gasset. Thus Romier lists youthfulness as one of the specifically American traits, while Maurois insists that "for many years there will still be 'a frontier' in America for those who are worthy of it." On the other hand, there are some European writers who prefer to describe the United States by the more uncomplimentary term "childish". Wyndham Lewis rubs salt into the wound by even suggesting that this nation is retrogressing to babyhood rather than remaining at a retarded level of development, while Odette Keun offers a slightly different approach in her assertion that America is immature. It is difficult to pass judgment on this characterization of the United States as youthful, since those thinkers holding this position generally arrive at their conclusion by intuition rather than logic, but this is also true of those who advocate the opposite view.

One of the leading exponents of the theory that America is essentially old is Amaury de Riencourt, who observes that "the triumph of machinery, the love of gadgets, the mechanization of the mind for the sake of comfort, always denote the oldster's outlook." De Riencourt also draws a parallel between the United States and Rome on the one hand and Europe and Greece on the other. In fact, it is most striking that those European commentators who consider this country mature or senile frequently set forth the same analogy as de Riencourt does. The Italian journalist Luigi Barzini, for example, insists that the United States is really an ancient European nation. There are, of course, those who straddle the fence on this issue. One may adopt either the approach of Andre Siegfried that the age of America is indeterminate or that of Hermann von Keyserling that it is both young and old. The question of whether American civilization is an extension of or a break with that of Europe has resulted in a rather similar division of opinion among writers abroad, as will be shown in the fourteenth chapter.

It was mentioned a few pages back that opinions about American individualism or conformism are often equated with those dealing with tolerance and intolerance. The charge of intolerance is particularly distasteful to Americans, especially since the principle of religious tolerance is written into the Constitution and a hostility towards intolerance is considered to be a concomitant of democracy. Hermann von Keyserling does believe that the development of a tolerant attitude in the United States "undoubtedly implies a high-water mark in human evolution up to the present," but this is quite definitely a minority opinion. Many European analysts, in fact, are as convinced that this nation is intolerant as they are that it is conformist.

As Hilaire Belloc observes, tolerance in America implies that one is allowed to do whatever he wishes to do *outside of* certain doctrines and practices to which he must adhere;[8] at best one has only partial freedom of action. M. J. Bonn also writes that American tolerance is based on the idea that everyone will automatically conform to "Americanism." It should be remembered, however, that pure tolerance has been a rarity in human history, and even that great proponent of tolerance, Jean Jacques Rousseau, was intolerant of those who were not tolerant. Consequently, it does seem a bit unfair for European writers to complain that Americans do not practice total tolerance when their homelands are no paragons of virtue in this respect. Perhaps, however, they are simply irritated at what they believe to be excessive claims on the part of this country that it is highly tolerant.

The three main forms that intolerance takes in the United States (or anywhere else) are the intellectual, religious, and racial. It is only to be expected that members of the European intelligentsia would be particularly disturbed by the first of these. As the English journalist Philip Gibbs observes, "in the United States, which is a real democracy . . . there is less toleration of eccentric notions than in England." Even Hermann von Keyserling, despite his remark of two paragraphs back, claims in a later work that the United States is becoming more intolerant as time goes on. Von Keyserling writes that "there is nothing less tolerant on earth than the spirit not only of the Ku Klux Klan and of Fundamentalism, but even of the Moralism of the small Middle-Western town." It would seem, however, that European commentators are in general less concerned with intolerance towards specific groups than they are with discrimination against the individual who acts and thinks differently from everyone else.

Another important consideration is whether Americans are opti-
mists or pessimists. There are some European thinkers, such as
Bernard Fay,[9] who do believe that there is a strong pessimistic element
in American life, but this view is not generally held; most European
writers label the United States as essentially optimistic, at least prior
to 1929. As might be expected, many Europeans stress the impact of
Rousseau on the intellectual history of this nation.

Analysts abroad are not always coldly objective, and many of them
view with envy and resentment those conditions in America which
stimulate the development of an optimistic spirit. As the Italian
historian Guglielmo Ferrero rather bitterly writes: "it is a state of
mind which sometimes irritates Europeans who know that all branches
of the human family did not receive . . . six and a half million
square miles of fabulously rich land to exploit." There is a widespread
belief abroad, moreover, that it is physical riches rather than human
ingenuity which is basically responsible for American "superiority".

European commentators often point out the inherent dangers in
the overly optimistic view of life which they believe particularly
characterizes this country. For example, Denis Brogan suggests that
American optimism may be disastrous in that it tends to deny reality,
while Jean-Paul Sartre remarks that this starry-eyed approach to life
makes it impossible for Americans to deal effectively with evil. But
it should be remembered that optimism is a characteristic of the
idealistic rather than the pragmatic element in American life; the
latter affords no basis for an optimistic outlook other than the success
of each particular act or series of actions. Another common European
criticism of the optimistic world view prevalent here is that it is a sign
of superficiality. Thus Richard Muller-Freienfels remarks "that the
profoundest joy may be tinged with sorrow, that the supremest
happiness may have an undertone of pain, is to him (the American)
incomprehensible."[10] Indeed, the very fact that this is an optimistic
nation is a proof of its immaturity to many European commentators,
as Europeans often stress that the pessimistic world view has been
the usual one during the last several millenia. An adherence to
an optimistic outlook therefore provides evidence that America
has experienced few of the difficulties and disasters that have beset
the path of humanity throughout history.

There are quite a few other American character traits of importance.
Since there appears to be no logical order in which to present them
the following arrangement is purely arbitrary. One of the more

striking of these is the lack of appreciation of leisure time or the inability to use it properly. This perhaps finds its tap root in the Puritan ethic of work; idleness was sinfulness according to the Puritans, although the presence of an excess of leisure is probably necessary for the development of an advanced culture. Lucien Romier asserts in this connection that "even to-day America seems to make the enjoyment of prolonged idleness irksome and embarrassing," while Bernard Fay declares that "far from enjoying its varied charms, leisure appears to them like a veritable Siva, a god of ruin." Jacques Maritain also observes that Americans have a horror of doing nothing, ostensibly much less concerned with being superficial than with being inactive. Consequently, one encounters here a constant striving, at times apparently after nothing, but still a striving and thus to the American mind an improvement over passivity.

Since this nation is constantly on the move, it is not unnatural that it is regarded abroad as dynamic. Thus Andre Siegfried observes that "the country still retains much of the full dynamism of the nineteenth century and at the same time has gained all the efficiency of the twentieth." English historian H. G. Wells similarly notes with approval the efforts of the New Deal in coping with the problem of limiting production in various fields, and this remark reflects the dynamic quality of the American economy. However, there are those Europeans, such as Harold Laski, who claim that America is characterized by restlessness rather than by dynamism. Moreover, Laski's correlation of this element with experimentalism is quite justified in that it has been borne out by the course of American history. It is true that Hermann von Keyserling maintains that the United States is less vital than Europe,[1] but such a belief is certainly not widespread abroad. Of course, Von Keyserling's theory that this country eventually will become static is quite tenable if one accepts the proposition that every nation is mortal and must eventually tend toward a lower state of energy.

A trait related to dynamism is enthusiasm. G. K. Chesterton observes that this "is where the American is fundamentally different" in that "to him the enthusiasm itself is meritorious." Chesterton does admit that to consider the American as the irresistible force and the Englishman as the immovable object is a vulgar oversimplification. Indeed, the fact that the American is so enthusiastic may in part explain why he is unable to use leisure time properly, as he converts his idle hours into work periods, rather than enjoying them in the manner that he should. Jacques Maritain points out in this connection that the active approach of the American often breeds impatience,[12] and thus it is only logical that this quality would accompany dynamism, enthusiasm, and an inability to use leisure time properly. As Denis Brogan observes, the history of the United States has been something of a success story; patience "is an un-American virtue, but one that is deeply necessary." It might be added that this impatient attitude is probably related to the American emphasis on the present. Americans generally do not live in the past or dream of an unattainable future as much as Europeans do.

A widespread belief also exists among Europeans that inarticulateness is the rule rather than the exception in the United States. Lucien Romier sympathetically suggests that "perhaps like many pathfinders or innovators who succeed in a great way, he (the American) doesn't know very well 'just how it was all done.'" Raymond Bruckberger similarly observes that this inarticulateness appears to be an "inability ... to make yourselves known for what you are" rather than a fault.[13] Since Americans often neglect to systematize their ideas and ideals, it is highly difficult for one to communicate their essence to foreigners, and this is one drawback of the pragmatic approach to life characteristic of this nation.

On the other hand, the typical American is frequently criticized because of his tendency to over-simplify and over-generalize. It would appear that this trait would be allied to a facile articulateness, although many contemporary writers do not seem to think so. Thus Luigi Barzini asserts that "travellers in the United States are at first pleasantly misled by the great wealth of oversimplified generalizations which have been fashioned (there)." Norman Angell similarly declares that Americans make cosmological prophecies on the most complex and involved issues imaginable in a naive, matter of fact manner. The positions which Romier and Barzini represent may appear to be irreconcilable, but it must be remembered that a dislike of generalizing is characteristic of American pragmatism, while an emphasis on generalizing is representative of American idealism.

Of the more positive character traits regarded abroad as representative of America, friendliness perhaps has made the strongest impression. Despite the fact that Simone de Beauvoir believes that Americans as a rule do not become deeply involved in love or friendship, G. K. Chesterton speaks of the Niagara of American sociability. Chesterton is probably more representative of European thought in this particular case. Of course, as George Bernard Shaw has pointed out, the social orientation of the American people is usually (if not invariably) correlated with a lack of privacy. This poses no difficulty at all to most Americans; a desire for privacy often is the result of having been accustomed to privacy. Thus if there has been no exposure, there is no need for it.

The fact that the United States functions more as a mass entity than as a collection of individuals furnishes proof to many Europeans that Americans are quite suggestible. Hermann von Keyserling traces this trait to the belief of the Behaviorist school of psychology that life is habit, and that habit is the result of external influences. Richard Muller-Freienfels, on the other hand, relates it to the impersonality of American life and the corresponding absence of depth and individuality. Perhaps a more fundamental explanation is that the American is in the fullest sense of the term a believer, and no matter whether the object of his worship is God, democracy, success or money he must believe in something.

In retrospect, it would appear that many of the elements of the American character, despite their seeming desirability (friendliness, for example), are tokens of a superficial rather than a profound world view. For this reason it is not surprising that Europeans take notice of the American tendency to evade the reality of death. Many of the great cultural milestones of civilization, from Homer's *Iliad* to Berlioz's *Requiem*, have made death the focal point of attention rather than ignoring the process of dying. In the United States today, however, one "passes away" rather than dies, and every attempt is made to prettify the end of earthly existence. As Luigi Barzini points out, "death is rouged, combed, and dressed by the undertakers, death is surrounded by the solemn and sanitary paraphernalia of medical science, death is barely mentioned in prayers and sermons." Simone de Beauvoir similarly observes that just about the only place in this country that one will encounter the reality of death is in cemeteries or funeral parks. Dying, of course, is the best argument there is against optimism (Heaven aside) and it may very well be significant that, like pessimism, it plays a less prominent role in American life than in European.

Those traits mentioned thus far in this chapter are probably the most significant ones analyzed by European commentators, but there are literally scores of others which are mentioned by them. As for the more negative features of the American character, Lucien Lehman chronicles such undesirable qualities as ignorance, brutality, egotism, dollar-philia, and immodesty in his *The American Illusion*. Lehman, of course, is so hostile to this country that it is easy to write

off his remarks as distorted and inaccurate. On the other hand, the
more objective Wyndham Lewis detects such flaws as sloth, hardness
(as contrasted to sensitivity), boastfulness, and over-politeness (which
sometimes takes the form of slyness.) Yet the logic that Lewis uses
to substantiate his ideas is not much of an improvement over that
of Lehman. From a general point of view, one might be surprised at
some of the more negative traits that European thinkers ascribe to
this country, such as the charge levelled by G. K. Chesterton that
Americans are not punctual. Others (boredom, for example) are
more consistent with the general train of criticisms directed against
this nation abroad.

The more positive American traits chronicled by observers in the
Old World constitute a veritable galaxy of elements as numerous
and diverse, if not more so, than that of the more negative ones. One
might mention here Andre Maurois' remarks on cheerfulness and
generosity, as well as Hermann von Keyserling's comments on sincerity and self-reliance. In addition, many others might be listed,
such as hospitality, adaptibility, and a lack of complaisance, and
these in general are those traits which most Americans like to believe are characteristic of us. There are, moreover, certain qualities
of a more ambiguous nature, in that to some European analysts they
are desirable while to others they are not. One might list here a lack
of nostalgia, sensuality, talkativeness, and an orientation towards the
future. As a result, if one were to attempt to make a classified
analysis in which each component of the American character was
to have its logical location, he would have considerable difficulty in
placing many of the above-mentioned traits in their proper niches.
Thus it becomes obvious why the present study has concentrated
on the few which Europeans generally regard as being most characteristic of this nation.

The best possible summation for this chapter would be a comparison of the American character with the European, but this is too
complex a subject to be dealt with here. Quite a few European critics
feel that such traits as individualism, maturity, and tolerance are more
typical of the Old World, while conformity, youthfulness, and bigotry
are more representative of the New. America is not, of course, a homogenous whole, and neither is Europe; hence it is extremely difficult for
one to make valid generalizations in regard to either. In addition,
conditions in the world today are in a state of flux and unrest; this is
what Saint-Simon would describe as a critical rather than an organic
period of history. Thus one must deal with an element of instability in

analyzing the character of any nation or continent, and this complicates matters.

As a final consideration, a distinction must be made between the American as he is today and as he was in the past or as he will be in the years to come. Although Philip Gibbs asserts that there is a representative American type, it is even more significant that Hermann von Keyserling writes of the American of the future as well as the American of the present.[14] For this reason, when one refers to the American character, it is absolutely necessary to qualify one's remarks by furnishing some sort of a chronological designation. Most commentators both here and abroad fail to supply this necessary information either through ignorance or oversight, and thus their observations are sometimes confusing. Each age, of course, has its own spirit, and this spirit so permeates every country that it makes a very strong impact on the national character. The soul of a nation, therefore, is never a constant quality, but is rather a becoming, and an analysis that ignores this dynamic factor constitutes a distortion of the facts. This, however, is exactly what far too many recent trans-Atlantic studies of the American character have turned out to be.

Chapter IV

POLITICS AND DEMOCRACY

The political life of the United States has probably received more attention from European commentators than any other topic. Such prominent writers as Denis Brogan and Harold Laski have, in fact, largely built up their reputations as leading authorities on this country through their analyses of American politics. It would be a mistake, however, to correlate such attention with approval, as there are many aspects of American political life which are viewed with a rather critical eye abroad. As a whole, the reaction of European critics to American politics might be characterized as slightly hostile rather than as highly favorable, although their attitude towards our brand of democracy is in general decidedly more positive. In the following analysis the majority of space is devoted to an examination of politics here, but this is for the reason that commentators abroad have written more on this subject than on the theoretical features of American democracy.

Of those aspects of our political life which have attracted the interest of European observers, the essentially non-ideological character of American political parties has perhaps aroused the most comment. Denis Brogan thus remarks that "American parties have never been bodies of men united on some general principles of government and united to put these principles into concrete form by legislation." The English journalist John St. Loe Strachey similarly writes that "indeed, it may be almost said that on the great issues there is a kind of unholy alliance between the competing parties to prevent any of the great moral or political problems (from) becoming the dividing line between parties," and other statements supporting this viewpoint might be listed *ad infinitum*.

Critics abroad also recognize for the most part that the old conservative versus liberal split is not the criterion separating the two major political organizations of the United States. As Andre Siegfried suggests, there have been such opposites as Calvin Coolidge and William Borah in the Republican Party and Alfred E. Smith and William Gibbs McAdoo in the Democratic. Americans see no overriding reason why political parties should not be administrative units rather than ideological vehicles, but many European observers apparently regard the American party set-up as bogus. At the same time, it is quite difficult for them to refute the fact that this nation enjoys greater political stability than many of those European countries in which the ideological cleavage dominates in politics. This is attested to by recent political failures in France.

Few foreign commentators go so far as to claim that there is a basic ideological difference between the Republican and Democratic Parties, but they often chronicle specific points on which there is a disagreement between them. Thus the Republican Party is generally associated in Europe with Big Business, a high tariff, and a strong central government, while the Democratic Party is linked with progressivism, the lower class, and states' rights. This division is complicated, however, by the fact that the New Deal brought about certain ideological switches, and the Democrats are now generally regarded as supporting centralization and the Republicans states' rights.

In addition, an examination of the earlier years of American history reveal other complicating factors. For example, the annexationist tendencies of the Democratic Party (especially its Southern wing) in the period prior to 1861 evolved into the anti-imperialist program which it espoused in 1900, while the anti-annexation philosophy prevalent among the Whigs in the 1840's developed into a policy of imperialism during the era of William McKinley and Theodore Roosevelt. Actually the only political parties in American history which have been characterized by firm ideological commitments have been the so-called "third" parties. But as Denis Brogan remarks, these "have never, except in the case of the Progressives in 1912, looked like having any chance of national success and, for the most part, died within an election or two after their birth." (The Republican Party was an exception to this rule.)

One encounters many stimulating theories as to why political parties in the United States have become essentially administrative rather than ideological. For example, Gunnar Myrdal suggests that there does not exist the sort of tie between political parties and social classes in America which might lead to divisions on sharply defined lines. On the other hand, Denis Brogan notes that the United States has become so complex that a national political party here must be "artificial" rather than meaningful in order to win votes and prosper. It also might be suggested that administration is today coming to play a larger and larger role in American life, so that it is only logical that American political parties would be "vast machines,"

as the English economist G. D. H. Cole describes them. This fact
is so obvious that it is often overlooked. Finally, as Denis Brogan
again observes, the old sectional attitudes of the parties are now
dying out in the United States; this development tends to eliminate
the only long-term point of division between the Republican and
Democratic Parties. Brogan's remark is borne out by Republican in-
roads into the South and Democratic successes in Northern New
England in recent elections.

Consequently, the stereotype prevalent in Europe of American
political parties is reflected in such observations as the English
economist Barbara Ward's remark that they have probably approached most nearly to the alternation of 'ins' and 'outs.'" Or, as Denis
Brogan suggests, they are "organized instrument(s) of securing consent" rather than ideological vehicles. There are, of course, a handful
of European thinkers, such as Harold Laski, who dream of a coming
political realignment in the United States in which the battle lines
will be drawn on the basis of issues. Such a prophecy is probably
based more on hope than on fact, and it is generally recognized
abroad that this nation is now moving away from the great ideological
battles of its past. It could be that this decline of the ideological
factor would result in the evolution of a watered-down version of the
totalitarian political organization of the type envisaged in George
Orwell's *1984*. European commentators, however, have neglected
this possibility, as they have focused their attention on such other
threats to American democracy as conformity resulting from social
pressures and standardization stemming from the techniques of mass
production.

Turning now to another aspect of the American political scene, it
will probably come as something of a shock that European critics
quite often characterize our politics as a reeking bog of graft and
corruption. Outspoken Odette Keun goes so far as to maintain
that "the Americans, probably three-fourths of whom are honest
and honorable in their private morals and life, become crooks the
moment they enter the political sphere."[15] Wyndham Lewis similarly
observes that "'graft' is an American word, again, and to be just
untidy about money is a characteristic of all administrations, except
the highest, in the U.S.A." One might cite numerous other comments
in support of this contention.

Although James Bryce once claimed that public opinion in this
country was less tolerant of abuses than it once had been, many
analysts both here and abroad would dispute his judgment today.

Thus Denis Brogan charges that corruption is a phenomenon characteristic of both urban and rural areas today. But at any rate, as the British historian Max Beloff points out, political corruption in America has not adversely affected the stability of this country. There exists a saying that a little honest graft is the grease which keeps the machinery of government in smooth operation, so that from the purely amoral point of view corruption may at times confer certain benefits.

European critics usually correlate the presence of corruption and graft with the existence of machine politics here, and the French writer Bertrand de Jouvenel notes in this connection that an American, Martin van Buren, was the inventor of the political machine. The technique of machine politics, of course, has been widely copied in Europe, and the adoption by Joseph Chamberlain of certain methods employed by Tammany Hall is a notable example of this imitation. While machine politics in the United States may be the result of democratic inertia,[16] as Denis Brogan suggests, it is usually accompanied by that phenomenon known as the spoils system.

Despite the fact that the merit system is not a cure-all, it unquestionably has numerous desirable attributes. In this connection Harold Laski justifiably predicts that the importance of the Federal civil service will probably increase in the years to come, while the "virus of patronage" will simultaneously wither away and die. As far as the lower levels of government are concerned, Denis Brogan suggests a joint reform of both city and state politics as the prerequisite of a long-range clean-up. Permanent reform is a difficult goal to attain; graft and corruption would not exist if there were not substantial tolerance of them on the part of the public.

Another striking conclusion that many European observers have reached is that the average office-holder in the United States is generally a man of mediocre ability. This generalization is usually conceived with reference to the period of American history since the advent of Jacksonian democracy drove the elite from public office. In support of this thesis J. A. Spender argues that "there is no country in the world in which so much energy, money, ingenuity and industry are devoted to public affairs, and none in which there seem to be so many obstacles to the steady pursuit of politics as a career for men of distinction." Lucien Lehman similarly states that "there is nothing to attract the better man and everything to repel him," as "talent . . . is a hindrance rather than an element of success." It is, of course, a fallacy to maintain that politicians are never chosen from among men of ability in this country. But, as Andre Siegfried suggests, members of the elite usually concentrate their efforts on the Congress, the various state governorships, and to a lesser extent, high ministerial positions. This quite obviously covers only a small portion of the governmental jobs, and able individuals are also needed at the lower levels.

The question may be raised as to why such a state of affairs exists in the United States. Denis Brogan suggests as an answer the fact that Americans do not regard the politician as being as "serious" as the business man or the professional man. Thus the gifted person hesitates to seek office here because he feels that he will not receive the measure of respect to which he is entitled. In addition, Harold Laski claims that the able American is not imbued with a sense of state and thus does not feel especially responsible for what his government does. Various other theories are also plausible. J. A. Spender, for example, maintains that the superior individual is unable to stomach the graft and corruption so characteristic of American politics today, while Lucien Lehman similarly observes that the person of ability is repulsed by the existence of political machines. It is, of course, quite difficult to refute these observations, as they are generally true, nor is one confidently able to offer ways of attracting the person of exceptional talents to governmental service. Still, it must be remembered that the American government has been quite successful in the past, regardless of the mediocre men who often have been in control of it.

Another significant generalization that foreign observers have reached is that the American public is only intermittently interested in politics. As a result, pressure groups are given the opportunity to play an important role in the governing of the country. Admittedly James Bryce once observed that "Public Opinion is, more fully than elsewhere, the ruling power" in the United States, but Andre Siegfried claims that "the main interest of the country is not political but is concentrated on production." Odette Keun seconds Siegfried's hypothesis in her assertion that the American tradition generally has been one of an anti-governmental and anti-executive character. It must be admitted, moreover, that up to the last quarter century or so there existed a widespread belief that the American government should interfere as little as possible in the life of the people.

In elaborating on the intermittent nature of political interest in America, Harold Laski writes that "public opinion is special and interested rather than general and disinterested." Yet one wonders if such an interest is continual even in a country which places a higher premium on politics. As for an exact determination of the cycle of political enthusiasm here, the one which European commentators generally accept is one with peaks every four years, with minor crests in between. Quite obviously these peaks correspond to Presidential election years, and M. J. Bonn claims with justification that these quadrennial eruptions of interest are the only times that Americans really become excited about politics. On the other hand, one questions the present applicability of the 1925 assertion of H. A. L. Fisher that the United States is "so happily sheltered by size and distance from external attack, that it can afford to neglect politics to an extent which would be dangerous in Europe." Still, it must be remembered that this country, unlike certain others, is characterized by relative political stability, and thus it probably would take a constant series of crises to keep the political temperature of the American people at continued fever pitch.

Consquently, it is not at all surprising that pressure groups would move into the political vacuum. The German economist Wilhelm Ropke goes so far as to assert that "this unwholesome development has probably reached its highest degree in the United States." Ropke also refers in his analysis to the innumerable lobbyists who have attached themselves to the American Congress as barnacles affix themselves to a ship. On the other hand, one must admit with Max Beloff that no one sectional or economic group is able to control or decidedly influence the policies of the American government, partly for the reason that these groups tend to cancel each other out. This does not lessen their significance in the slightest; they remain distinctly important forces in the life of this nation. Indeed, as Oswald Spengler points out in *The Decline of the West,* the presence and activity of pressure groups (especially the economic ones) tends to deflect the attention of the nation from purely political matters. But thinkers abroad have remained strangely silent in regard to solutions to this problem, perhaps because they have no panaceas, perhaps because they are pointedly aware of the existence of similar groups (such as the Catholic Church) in their own homelands. They certainly realize that such organizations may not be made to disappear simply by waving one's pen at them, as they obviously fulfill a need, or else they would not exist.

The focal point of this chapter now shifts to an examination of the highly significant subject of American democracy. Such a prominent European thinker as Jacques Maritain contends that the United States is the outstanding democratic regime in the world, while G. K.

Chesterton observes that it is the only nation that was ever founded on a creed.[17]   Although one must agree with Wilhelm Ropke that the Founding Fathers had certain reservations about democracy being adopted *in toto,* this does not alter the fact that the democratic element was present in American life from the very first.   Democracy has, however, reached the stage in this country where some critics claim that it has become practically enshrined as a religion.   As Raymond Bruckberger writes, "for every American, democracy is an absolute that has the sacred and intangible value of myth."   Thus to question its basic assumptions here is almost as unthinkable as it would be to cast doubt on the Christian faith in Europe during the Middle Ages.

This does not mean that European thinkers are never critical of American democracy, as such eminent analysts as James Bryce have frequently pointed out its faults.   Hermann von Keyserling notes one of the most important of these in his remark that "what is required if democracy in America is to become again a progressive element in the human, as opposed to the merely technical sense . . . is *that diversity and manifoldness should henceforth be stressed more than anywhere else in the world.*"   Other criticisms might also be noted, but the majority of them are variations on this theme.

Most historians, both here and abroad, accept the theory that the stream of American democracy has exerted its force through two channels, the Jeffersonian and the Hamiltonian.   In its pure form Jeffersonianism stressed the fundamental goodness of man and the desirability of limited government.   On the other hand, Hamiltonianism emphasized the importance of protecting the individual from society and the necessity of a strong central authority.   It unquestionably would have been disastrous if either had been totally victorious at the expense of the other, since each has its characteristic faults.   Thus Wyndham Lewis observes that "Jeffersonian democracy contains much more that is anarchial than democratic," while Odette Keun complains that Hamilton "did not care for humanity and he did not care for equity."   Both of these claims are somewhat exaggerated, but they point up the fact that American democracy is a synthesis of seemingly irreconcilable opposites.

In regard to the struggle for supremacy between these two great traditions, Barbara Ward asserts that from the economic point of view Hamiltonianism was victorious in America after the Civil War, while Odette Keun writes that in the case of political ideals Jeffersonianism has triumphed. Bertrand Russell concurs in both of these penetrating observations. Of course, there are such dissenters as Wyndham Lewis who maintain that "all American politicians today are in theory Jeffersonian, in practice Hamiltonian," but such a belief is an expression of a minority opinion. Most European thinkers of prominence are as aware as their American counterparts that both of these traditions play an integral role today in the life of this nation, although their relative strengths may vary from time to time.

With this background in mind, the stage is set for an examination of the relationship of democracy to American life. This discussion will begin with a reference to the compatibility of democratic ideals and economic controls, a problem which has engendered considerable disagreement among foreign commentators. On the one hand, Austrian economist Ludwig von Mises charges that total governmental control of business is ultimately incompatible with any form of constitutional and democratic government. On the other, Gunnar Myrdal insists that democracy and free enterprise must solve the problem of full employment together, while Harold Laski even claims that there exists an "inherent contradiction between capitalism and democracy." Denis Brogan sums the situation succinctly in his observation that "the problem facing all the democratic countries today (especially the United States) is the reconciliation of political democracy with economic development." Quite obviously this dilemma has not been resolved in a universally acceptable manner, mainly for the reason that capitalists, New Dealers, and socialists hold differing views as to the extent that the government should interfere in the economy.

From the social point of view the implications of democracy are likewise of significance. André Siegfried reflects a common American sentiment in his claim that a social democracy is developing in the United States, but many European commentators regard the treatment of the American Negro as something of a scandal. Moreover, critics here at times ignore the fact that a relationship exists between the social makeup of the population and the form which democracy takes, while those abroad frequently stress it. Thus Oswald Spengler draws a correlation between the absence of yeomanry from America and the existence of democracy, while Salvador de Madariaga asserts that this country is really a "burgess" democracy because of its lack of a peasant class. Equally consequential, for all practical purposes, is the stress M. J. Bonn places on the agrarian element and the English historian Geoffrey Barraclough on the urban proletariat in the evolution of American democracy, as these thinkers occupy positions roughly analogous to those held here by Frederick Jackson Turner and Arthur Schlesinger, Jr. These examples indicate that the social aspects of democracy, like the economic, are often a matter of controversy abroad, perhaps because Europeans are more class conscious than are Americans.

The question of whether democracy and equality have become synonymous here also merits attention. This issue is of great significance in that it involves an evolution of the concept of democracy from an emphasis on the political rights of the individual to a stress on general equality. As for those who take an affirmative position, Richard Muller-Freinfels maintains that America has been transformed from a democracy of liberty into one of equality,[18] while Hermann von Keyserling insists that "if democracy is taken to mean equality, then there is indeed more . . . in the United States than anywhere else in the West." A majority of European critics recognize that such an evolution has taken place, but many "purists" claim that the current definition of democracy is a perversion of its original meaning.

Another pertinent consideration is whether liberalism and democracy in America should be regarded as contradictory rather than complimentary. M. J. Bonn claims that the two concepts are incompatible in that "liberalism by its very essence demands personal freedom as the supreme good," while "democracy, based as it is on the notion of a community, may use force in the interests of the commonweal." All American liberals claim that they believe in democracy, but conservative critics abroad often charge that their liberalism is of a bogus variety. Such European leftists as Harold Laski sometimes attempt to resolve this question by equating socialism with liberalism, maintaining that socialism and democracy are compatible. But this does not provide a satisfying answer to a rather thorny problem: the liberal tradition has taken different forms in the Old World than it has in the New.

European commentators are also in disagreement as to whether or not the American democratic way of life should become the way of life of the entire planet. On the one hand, M. J. Bonn maintains that American democracy by its very nature must spread itself over the whole globe,[19] while the English historian Alfred Zimmern writes that we must fortify liberty all over the world in order to secure the blessings of liberty to ourselves. Both of these theories are linked to the theory that since democracy is dynamic, it must either expand or lose its vigor, a hypothesis which also has been advanced in regard to communism. In contrast, Andre Siegfried observes that the

American system is probably not suited to universal application, and Norman Angell goes even further in asserting that the United States should not try to force democracy on the rest of the globe. The fact comes to mind, however, that less than a century ago the leading countries of Europe forcibly spread European civilization over the backward areas of the world. Just to what degree, therefore, European disapproval of the American attempt to democratize the whole planet is based on resentment, and to what extent it is founded on valid grounds is uncertain. Foreigners, however, rarely go so far as to implore the United States to keep its ideals to itself, but instead suggest that it should practice moderation.

It thus seems that the two topics which have been treated in this chapter offer totally contrasting pictures of American life. There are many European critics who may react to the material presented here by charging that it reflects the basic hypocrisy of the American people; at least from a superficial point of view it would appear that this accusation is justified. But it should be remembered that political activity is an aspect of the realistic approach to life, while democratic theory is a phase of the idealistic. Consequently, it is probable that these seemingly opposing elements are simply different sides of the same coin rather than incompatible opposites. Otherwise, political realities and democratic ideals would not be able to function side by side in the United States. It will be shown in the following chapter that the government is the instrument by which this act has been affected, as principle and practice meet here in, if not perfect, at least workable harmony. Commentators abroad have frequently maintained that American desires have outrun American abilities, but it would appear that the Founding Fathers were able to steer a middle course between the excesses of these two extremes.

CHAPTER V

THE CONSTITUTION IN THEORY AND PRACTICE

The American Constitution long has been an object of fascination to European observers. This is not only because Americans regard it as holy, but also because of the attempts which Charles A. Beard and his followers have made to bring it down from Mount Olympus to a more earthly level.

In regard to the sanctified nature of this document, French journalist Raymond Aron refers to it as possessing "an almost mystical prestige, while Denis Brogan describes it as a "national tailsman."[20] One could easily list here dozens of similar characterizations. Although Oswald Spengler traces this reverence to a general worship of traditional forms in times of trouble, John St. Loe Strachey asserts that this deification is potentially dangerous in that the Constitution is too rigid to meet the demands of a changing society. However, both writers miss the mark in that the Constitution has been hallowed throughout American history both in peace and peril, and has been flexible enough to meet every crisis thus far.

At one time a belief was current both here and abroad that the Constitution was the work of radical libertarians who were fanatically devoted to the establishment of a new order. This cherished hypothesis was smashed beyond repair around the time of World War I by the late Charles A. Beard, who demonstrated that the document was the work of the wealthier class. An extremist reaction to this discovery is the claim of Bertrand Russell that "the adoption of the Constitution was the first step in building up the political power of the plutocracy."[21] But despite the revelation that the Founding Fathers were indeed as close to the Bourbons as to the Jacobins, they nevertheless have retained their exalted status as public idols here. As the French journalist Raoul de Roussy de Sales remarks, "contemporary Americans have a tendency to attribute to the Fathers of the Constitution some sort of superhuman power."

Fortunately, the fact that the framers of the document are no longer regarded as wild-eyed reformers has resulted in a re-examination of the conservative features of the Constitution both here and abroad. In this connection one might cite such brakes on radicalism as the separation of powers principle, the electoral college system, and an independent Supreme Court. As Amaury de Riencourt points out, the Founding Fathers designed a document which would serve as a counterbalance to the state legislatures, which often were controlled by insolvent debtors. For this reason, the basic philosophy underlying the Constitution should be regarded as conservative in that it stresses property rights and fiscal responsibility.

It is not unexpected that many foreign commentators would not approve of certain aspects of the Constitution. For example, Arnold Toynbee criticizes this document on the grounds that it guards against dictatorships but not against personal exploitation. It is, therefore, not surprising that thinkers abroad have suggested various Constitutional reforms. Thus Harold Laski proposes that the Electoral College be eliminated, the President be allowed an unlimited number of terms, the chief executive be given the right of partial veto, treaties be ratified by a simple majority of both houses of Congress, and the powers of the Supreme Court be reduced. Quite a few other European critics have offered similar proposals, such as Denis Brogan's suggestion that the terms of the members of the House of Representatives be increased from two to four years, but a cataloguing of all of them would take up a prohibitive amount of space.

This discussion now shifts to an examination of the three branches of the national government established by the Constitution. Here the Executive will be dealt with first, since it is the branch to which Europeans tend to be the most sympathetic. Many maintain that a strong President is a good President, and it is quite significant that the extension of the functions of the Presidential office by such a man as Abraham Lincoln does not meet with very much censure abroad. Similarly, it is not surprising that the President is often compared to a hereditary ruler by some European writers. For example, G. K. Chesterton remarks that "it is the President who ought to be called King," while Max Beloff pictures Dwight Eisenhower as the equal of a constitutional monarch. Accordingly, there perhaps was more truth than fancy in the labeling of Franklin Roosevelt as Roosevelt II by many writers both here and abroad.

An examination of those qualities which European critics regard as hallmarks of an ideal President reveals that the image which emerges is one of power rather than of docility. Thus James Bryce writes that "that which most attracts the people is the thing we call a Strong Personality," and Bryce regards such traits as courage, energy, intellectual power, cleverness, and command of language (but not

wisdom or eloquence) as being desirable for a President. Bryce emphasizes, moreover, that these qualities must be so synthesized as to
present a unified image rather than remaining separate. But perhaps
even more important, as Harold Laski points out, is the ability of a
President to choose and handle men. Laski maintains that F. D. R.
possessed this quality, while both Lincoln and Wilson largely lacked
it. In addition, the President must be a master politician, a fact which
perhaps was lost sight of during the Eisenhower Administration.
Thus H. G. Wells states that "how it could be possible to become
President of this United States and not be a politician, no one has ever
explained to me." Wells further comments that it is not enough for
the President to be a "good fellow" (as was Harding) or "a paralyzed
figurehead overcome by his own prominence" (as was Hoover).[22]

When relations between the President and Congress are strained,
observers abroad usually take the side of the President. In this connection James Bryce has pointed out that the President and not
Congress is the center of American political life. M. J. Bonn adds
that the President, and not Congress, puts the will of the people
into action. Harold Laski similarly observes that it is the President
who gets the blame if things go wrong. Laski also detects a growth in
the power of the Executive branch of the government at the expense
of that of the Legislative, and even suggests that the President should
be given more initiative in handling crucial international situations.
It is perhaps ironical that European political writers are generally in
favor of increasing the power of the President, since it has been the
Legislative rather than the Executive branch of the govrnment which
has been the guardian of democracy throughout history If either has
usurped authoritarian power here it has been the President, with the
single important exception of Reconstruction, but this does not deter
foreign critics from occasionally advocating an encroachment by
the Executive branch upon the power of Congress.

Perhaps the most condemned feature of the American Presidency is
the manner in which the President is nominated and elected. If
European critics are correct in their criticisms of the electoral process,
it is quite surprising that any one of ability ever reaches the highest
political office of the land. Denis Brogan complains that reform is
needed even in the method of selecting delegates to the national
conventions, since the people often do not have a voice in choosing
them. As for the conventions, Harold Laski asserts that the Presidential candidate is often selected on the grounds of "least offensive-
ness," while Bertrand Russell maintains that the candidate is fre-

quently colorless and lacking in magnetism. In regard to the election, Laski compares it to a lottery, quoting the remark of Walter Bagehot that success in such a form of gambling is no argument for the method. Denis Brogan also points out that the present electoral set-up has at times resulted in the election of a candidate by a minority of the popular vote, and it must be admitted that this criticism was borne out by the 1960 election.

A concise summary of the general oveseas evaluation of certain Presidents might prove enlightening at this point in the narrative. Europeans generally consider George Washington to be a great man, but they regard Thomas Jefferson rather than Andrew Jackson as the epitome of democracy. Abraham Lincoln is, of course, so complex a figure that it is difficult to generalize about him other than to note that he is one of the leading personifications of the American way of life. In the more recent period of American history, Theodore Roosevelt rates fairly high on the other side of the Atlantic, despite his rebuffs to England and Germany in the Venezuelan debt controversy and his part in the Spanish-American war. On the other hand, Woodrow Wilson does not fare so well, since both his foreign and his domestic policies have been attacked abroad.

As for the triumvirate of Republicans who ruled this country during "Normalcy," Warren Harding and Calvin Coolidge are generally regarded in Europe as lightweights in that they did not exert strong Presidential leadership. But Herbert Hoover, despite his failure in dealing with the depression of 1929, ranks much higher, probably because of his activities before and after he was President. Most European critics regard in a favorable manner Franklin Roosevelt, Harry Truman, and Dwight Eisenhower, mainly because all three helped to implement the partnership between America and the democracies of Europe. Consequently, one might conclude that the American Presidency is now looked upon with an unusual degree of approval in Europe, but this should be attributed to the men holding the office in recent years as much as to the office itself.

In contrast, Congress seems to be the least admired abroad of the three branches of the national government. An element of hostility is present in a great many of the remarks of European critics, and this negative bias must be kept in mind here while evaluating their observations. Thus Bernard Fay charges that Congress "feels an instinctive aversion for Europe, a lively distaste for any brilliant adventure and an invincible suspicion of every intellectual and ideological scheme." Fay also remarks that Congress "bears in mind the

multitudinous small interests of the small folk or small groups" rather
than concerning itself with more important considerations. From
a more sympathetic point of view, Denis Brogan admits that Congress
is often the victim of a bad press in America as well as in Europe. The
fact remains, however, that such past incidents as the Senate's
rejection of the Treaty of Versailles has not endeared Congress to
Europeans. Moreover, this rejection unquestionably has impaired
our rapport with the Old World far more than considerations such as
the existence of certain technical differences between the American
Congress and European legislative bodies.

It was pointed out in the last chapter that a widespread belief is
prevalent in Europe that mediocrity is generally characteristic of the
American politician. This trait is regarded as being more representative of the Legislative than it is of the Executive or Judicial
branches, although this is not always the case. In writing of the
lack of exceptional ability of Congressmen, Harold Laski acidly
observes that "the proper commentary upon the system is the simple
fact that most congressmen are unsuccessful lawyers." James Bryce
similarly notes that "they are citizens little above their fellows in
knowledge and intellectual gifts." Harold Laski has even criticized
the Congressional system itself, while Denis Brogan and other European commentators have suggested various reforms, such as the
establishment of closer ties between Congress and the President. Most
of the recommendations, however, are so complex that it is impossible
to deal with them here, even in summary form. One, of course,
should distinguish between those proposals advocating an increase in
the efficiency of Congress, which are universally supported in Europe,
and those calling for a modification in the powers of Congress, which
have been received with mixed feelings.

The writings of European critics are also of interest in that they
reflect a differing estimate of the House of Representatives and the
Senate, both in the general level of ability of the membership and the
contributions to American life of each. Although the House of Representatives is probably closer to the ideal of a purely democratic body
than is the Senate, it is usually regarded abroad as being inferior to
the upper house in most respects. In this connection the reference
of Denis Brogan to its "comparatively infrequent debates" and "its
rigorous procedure" is representative. Brogan also remarks that
"the fame of a leading member of the House of Representatives is
... the fame of a master of guerrilla warfare." In contrast, the Senate
has been evaluated more favorably in Europe, and has been praised

even by Harold Laski as an outstanding success. Laski thus asserts that the Senate "transcends the sectionalism which pervades every nook and cranny of the House of Representatives," as well as being "perhaps the most vital check upon the despotism an ambitious president could so easily develop." Admittedly European observers do not always contrast the two bodies as vividly as the above examples might indicate, but they rarely rank them on the same level.

In regard to the Judicial branch, the Supreme Court presents a paradox in that it is highly admired abroad, yet many of its actions have met with rather sharp disapproval. In analyzing the American idolization of the Supreme Court, Bertrand Russell remarks that "in the United States at the present day, the reverence which the Greeks gave to oracles and the Middle Ages to the Pope is given to the Supreme Court." Bertrand de Jouvenel also notes that "in this institution the Americans have found the bulwark of their liberty and the dam to Power's encroachments." It appears, therefore, that some of the deification accorded the Constitution here has "rubbed off" on the Supreme Court. However, one encounters very few criticisms of this judicial body on the grounds that Americans view it in a pious manner, as European thinkers are far more disturbed because it is swayed by extra-legal considerations at times.

Two leading European critics of the Supreme Court are Harold Laski and Denis Brogan, both of whom occupy a position left of center politically. Laski and Brogan accuse the Supreme Court of promoting the interests of the more conservative elements of this nation, and they are especially critical of the manner in which the Supreme Court has interpreted the Fourteenth Amendment. Laski thus writes that "anyone who, in the United States, takes the history of the Fourteenth Amendment can hardly help insisting that the Courts have been the instrument of business men in their fight against the development of social legislation." Brogan similarly maintains that this amendment "made possible and easy the transformation of the Supreme Court into a third chamber voting legislation on grounds of policy." Both of these observations are borne out by history, as it is recognized by most historians that Roscoe Conkling offered an interpretation of the Fourteenth Amendment in 1882 which made it a protective shield for the propertied interests. This interpretation was not effectively challenged until this century, and even then it was not jettisoned without a struggle. In addition, both Brogan and Laski accuse the Supreme Court of mixing in politics, although one

wonders what their reaction would have been if it had taken the side
of the political left more often.

The Supreme Court crisis during the middle 1930's quite naturally
is the focal point of attention abroad. Thinkers of the ideological
bent of Laski and Brogan invariably castigate the Supreme Court,
although more moderate observers such as Bertrand de Jouvenel and
Philip Guedalla affirm that both sides were at fault. In addition.
there is a surprising amount of interest in Europe in the decline of
stare decisis (respect of past precedents) as a factor in Supreme Court
decisions. On the one hand, Max Beloff writes that "it is fortunate
for the United States that the Supreme Court has never had the
English respect for the principle of *stare decisis*," for a rigid adherence
to its decisions would have hindered the growth of a dynamic society
here. In contrast, Denis Brogan remarks that "the increasing readi-
ness of the Court to admit changing its mind does weaken the prestige
of the system," so that there is a disagreement abroad as to whether
a reliance on *stare decisis* is desirable or not. One might suggest that
current European attitudes towards the Supreme Court are perhaps
more complex and divided than they ever have been, but these differing opinions are, of course, the result of its decisions rather than of
its prestige.

Having analyzed the various components of the national government in isolation, an examination of the role that it plays as a whole
in American life is in order. The fundamental question here is whether
there is an increasing concentration of power in the hands of the
national government, and if so, whether such a concentration is
desirable or not. In this connection, the ideas of Harold Laski are
of significance since they reflect a pro-statist point of view. On the one
hand, he writes of the emergence of the "Positive State" in America
during the administration of Franklin Roosevelt, but on the other
hand, Laski admits that the present system does not delegate enough
power to the national government to guarantee social reform.[23]

Although Laski is essentially thinking in terms of domestic affairs,
Oswald Spengler expresses similar sentiments in the international
sphere. Thus Spengler questions the desirability of the separation of
powers concept in his remark that "the parallelism of President and
Congress which she (America) derived from a theory of Montesquieu
has, with her entry into world politics, become untenable." Even
such a foe of a strong central government as Ludwig von Mises admits that the control of business must be partially in the hands of the
national government. Of course, von Mises is hardly in favor of

unlimited governmental tampering with the system of free enterprise, but he does recognize that a certain amount of governmental supervision is absolutely mandatory.

In contrast, many European commentators have spoken out in favor of decentralization in America, including Harold Laski, who grudgingly admits that to an extent this is a necessity in the United States. Thus Laski writes that "the attempt to govern territories as diverse as Arizona and New York by uniform methods would be fraught with disaster." In comparing the national government of the United States with that of France, Andre Maurois similarly remarks that the former "has nothing in common . . . with a single focus of power like the Government in Paris." Maurois also points out that there is no national Minister of Education in the United States as there is in many European countries. Even more significant is the assertion of Philip Guedalla that "authority has been fragmented (in America) with such ingenuity that no one could lay hands on it," for "if sovereignty resided anywhere in the United States, it lay beyond the Constitution in the broad masses of the people." This observation brings into focus the difficulties involved in consolidating the power of the national government at the expense of that of the state and the populace. Consequently, even if it is admitted that there is a movement in America away from decentralization, such a movement still has many obstacles to overcome before it reaches its goal.

The fact remains, however, that a vast administrative bureaucracy is being created in Washington through both the Civil Service and the spoils system. One significant feature of the development of this "fourth" branch of the national government is that it is protected by an increasing number of regulations and ordinances. Therefore, it has become rather difficult for the other branches of the government to control its growth. Although Hilaire Belloc writes that the idea of a governing class is alien to the average American, and Ludwig von Mises asserts that America is only superficially afflicted with bureaucracy, there is an awareness abroad that such a bureaucratic elite is slowly evolving in Washington.

Despite the large number of governmental workers employed in this country, however, the German economist Joseph Schumpeter and Gunnar Myrdal have charged that the bureaucracy centered in the nation's capitol is inefficient. A typical proposal remedying this situation is that of Harold Laski, who suggests that a secretariat be created so as to facilitate relations between the Executive and the other branches of the national government. But although it is often of mediocre quality, one still has to agree with Laski and Denis Brogan that administration plays the major role in governmental life today. Moreover, there is not much chance of eliminating the bureaucracy that has developed, only one of keeping it in check, since its annihilation would be as disastrous as its mushrooming.

In regard to state and local government, the consensus abroad appears to be that they have not carried out their functions as well as they should have. On the other hand there exists an awareness that they are a necessary evil. Thus Denis Brogan notes that the states have declined in importance in recent years, but he strongly affirms that the state system should not be discarded. Brogan, however, admits that the concept of states' rights is not observed when it is in the interest of a state to neglect it, and this criticism is especially valid in the field of civil rights. Various European thinkers who favor a strong central government, such as Harold Laski, do maintain that the present division of America into states should be abolished, but they are apparently in the minority, as there exists an awareness abroad that the partition of power between the national and state governments serves as a check against totalitarianism.

As for specific criticisms of state and local government, one might mention Denis Brogan's condemnation of American state courts, "whose powers have often been a good deal in excess of their capacities." Brogan also finds both state and municipal taxing systems to be "archaic and absurd." Similarly, James Bryce notes that city government in this country is a failure, since municipal affairs "have furnished the most striking illustrations of dangers inherent to democracy." Harold Laski, on the other hand, complains that local governmental units here are irresponsible in the legal sense. On occasion one will find a few lukewarm words of praise, such as the declaration of Denis Brogan that American police are better than it is generally thought, but even such a grudging compliment as this is decidedly the exception to the rule. It is noteworthy that European observers generally recommend a drastic over-all reform rather than suggest specific proposals, as this reveals that many of them regard state and local government here to be in a rather hopeless state.

In closing, it is desirable to make a few observations on the position of the American people under the Constitution which will serve as a supplement to the material presented in the last chapter. Most observers abroad recognize that the government here is run in accordance with their wishes when they really exert themselves, and Philip Gibbs even complains that majority rule assumes a tyrannical character at times. This claim is perhaps not wholly unjustified. In addition, it is generally acknowledged in Europe that freedom of speech exists in this country in fact as well as in theory. Admittedly one encounters complaints such as the one of the English economists Sidney and Beatrice Webb that the monied interests are able to stifle this freedom in the United States on occasion,[24] but it must be remembered that freedom of speech never has been exercised in an absolute form anywhere.

As far as personal liberty in America is concerned, there is a bit more disagreement. Thus Harold Laski complains that liberty is not always accompanied by equality of opportunity, while Lucien Romier laments because many individuals interpret liberty as the license to engage in social and economic activities without political interference. There is, of course, no guarantee that one will use his liberty in a socially constructive manner, although this is certainly desirable. But despite the fact that Andre Siegfried fears that social conformity will eventually undermine liberty in this country, Denis Brogan points out an important truth when he observes that the American citizen has more freedom from the legal point of view than he does in Europe. One might therefore conclude (and most European thinkers would agree) that Americans rarely exercise their rights in a perfect manner, but the stumbling blocks that they encounter are far outnumbered by the advantages which they enjoy under the Constitution.

CHAPTER VI

CAPITALISM AND ITS CRITICS

The economic factor has certainly been a key one in the historical growth of this nation. Norwegian historian Halvdan Koht is among those who feel that "American development helped strengthen and confirm the economic interpretation of history."[25] Thus the United States is often cited abroad as one of the most convincing proofs that the economic element has been fundamental in the development of world civilization. On the other hand, as Arnold Toynbee and other European writers point out, the United States was economically "the child of Western Europe" to 1914. The French economist Ernest Teilhac similarly observes that economic theory in Nineteenth Century America was strongly influenced by trends then current across the Atlantic. It would seem, therefore, that the singling out of America as the embodiment of the capitalist tradition is an exaggeration.

Although most foreign thinkers admit the United States surpasses Europe from the point of view of quantitative output, there exists a widespread sentiment that the material resources of this country are being wasted, and some commentators even maintain that this recklessness poses a danger to the nation's economy. As Georges Duhamel writes, America has been plundered rather than loved or beautified, while Sidney and Beatrice Webb refer to "the devastation and destruction of the natural resources of the American continent." Odette Keun even goes so far as to claim that the physical riches of this country will be exhausted unless something is done about it. It may be true, as Arnold Toynbee points out, that this tendency to use recklessly the natural resources of the land "is characteristic of our Western world as a whole" and not just the United States, but this is obviously no justification for the excesses which have been committed here.

Although both Toynbee and Bertrand Russell maintain that it is the physical rather than the human factor that is exploited in the United States, many European critics react to the decimation of forests and fields here as if human souls were being slaughtered in the process. Harold Laski, moreover, raises the question of the distribution of these physical riches in his remark that "the problem of

58

planning the use of American resources for the total good of the community" must be solved. Despite the fact that not every critic would agree with Laski as to the means by which this is to be effected, there seems to be a general agreement abroad that it is not desirable for a handful of individuals to hoard the natural resources of the land.

Obviously the mere presence of an abundance of physical riches in itself does not account for American economic ascendancy, as many other factors also are of importance. The absence of internal economic barriers doubtless ranks first in a listing of these, and Norman Angell even maintains that Europe would be as rich as America if a universally free market existed there. Barbara Ward similarly declares that the efficacy of mass production could only have been proved in a country with a free market such as the United States. Although such European commentators as Gunnar Myrdal have attacked the protective tariff on various grounds, both Andre Siegfried and Lucien Romier recognize that it has had a beneficial effect on mass production here. While Romier also mentions the recent erection of tariff barriers within the British Empire, it must be remembered that free trade has triumphed in the United States at the expense of protectionism in 1933.

These two factors just dealt with are probably the most important ones, but others also merit attention. For example, Guglielmo Ferrero notes that America has waxed fat with riches because the upper classes "instead of spending their enormous incomes on pleasure alone, invested the larger part in new enterprises." In addition, the French journalist Andre Lafond writes of American *élan* as a factor in the economic success of this country, while Ludwig von Mises concludes that the superiority of American tools was responsible for the increase in American productivity. Although Lafond tends to downgrade the latter factor, both spirit and technique have been of importance in economic development here. A favorite of American capitalists is the hypothesis of von Mises that the United States is more prosperous than other nations because "their government embarked later than the government in other parts of the world upon the policy of obstructing business." Such proponents of governmental control of the economy as Harold Laski often take issue with this theory, but it appears to be the consensus abroad (aside from the socialists) that von Mises' assertion is valid.

The focal point of this narrative now shifts to an examination of the system of free enterprise currently in operation in the United States. This subject is especially controversial, as a wide range of economic philosophies characterize the body of writings which were examined in researching this monograph. One rather striking fact is that it is often the spokesmen of the economic Left rather than the economic Right who most strongly stress the degree to which capitalism is entrenched in the United States. For example, G. D. H. Cole writes that "this system and this structure are almost unchallenged" in America, while M. J. Bonn observes that America "is the only great country in the world which has evolved a system of 'undiluted' capitalism." On the other hand, H. G. Wells and Denis Brogan both write of the decline and collapse of rugged individualism in the United States, and they are not alone in their pessimistic judgments.

From a more moderate point of view, Barbara Ward asserts that "most Americans believe strongly in the free enterprise system but few of them are confident that it has found any solution for the recurring crises of depression and unemployment." This is probably a more reasonable conclusion. Significant in this connection is the claim of Harold Laski that capitalism must succeed in this nation or fail on a worldwide scale, as it brings into focus the international ramifications of the capitalist system. Although there are those European commentators, such as Raymond Bruckberger, who do write that the American concept of free enterprise may be the answer to the world's problems, this is not a universally held opinion. Also in evidence are such remarks as the one of Denis Brogan that "free enterprise of the American type may be a luxury that some countries cannot afford," and it appears that the success of the capitalist system in the United States is no guarantee that it will be welcomed abroad with open arms.

Mass production[26] and American capitalism are correlated in the minds of many European observers, despite the fact that they are not necessarily adjuncts. It is paradoxical that American mass production is criticized abroad because it leads to a quantitative rather than a qualitative approach to life, yet is also praised because it tends to raise the standard of living of the masses. The first of these points is stressed throughout this volume, especially in the twelfth chapter, but the second is also important. However, one does not meet it as often in the observations of European thinkers, quite possibly for the reason that many of the latter do not care to admit its truth. The main argument in favor of mass production in America is, of course, that it provides a firm basis for economic democracy, and this is a fact which socialists find particularly distasteful. But the latter group rarely meet the issue head-on; they usually fall back on the old argument that goods may be plentiful in the United States but they are also of an inferior quality.[27] This charge is made in the face of the fact that the remainder of the world is converting to mass production as rapidly as possible, but European critics are not always noted for their consistency.

To most Europeans Wall Street is the embodiment of American capitalism. Despite the fact that the intellectual elite is far more sophisticated than the sometimes Communist influenced masses, the assertions of commentators abroad in regard to it often display an alarming naivete. Thus Lucien Lehman reflects a stereotyped view in his declaration that "the mountaineers of Tennessee, the farmers of Kansas, the prospectors of Arizona, no matter how ignorant or primitive in ideas they may be, all know that there exists somewhere on the American continent a Money Mecca, and that the name of that holy place is Wall Street." Although Lehman's remark may be dismissed as the rantings of a bigot, it is difficult to overlook certain observations of the more profound European analysts. The English economist John Maynard Keynes, for example, notes (in *The General Theory of Employment, Interest, and Money,* of all places) that "when the capital development of a country becomes a by-product of the activities of a casino, the job is likely to be ill-done." Doubtless this rather frigid reception of Wall Street in Europe is partly due to envy and resentment, for as Bertrand Russell states, "the dislike of America which has grown up in England is due to the fact that world empire has now passed from Lombard Street to Wall Street." But even this fact hardly accounts for bizarre characterizations of Wall Street conceived by some of Europe's most brilliant minds.

The American business man also has come in for his share of diatribes abroad. There are probably few more totally misinformed remarks than the one of Harold Laski that business men "keep on" good football or baseball players in high school here by means of financial support. Laski also refers to the narrow outlook on life so characteristic of many American business leaders. Various American qualities or traits are, of course, unfavorably regarded abroad, and one of the more distasteful of these is the business man's "cut-throat" competitiveness. Thus M. J. Bonn writes that "competition in American business life is different from the rivalry with which an aristocratic society is familiar, a rivalry originating in sport, and restricted from the beginning by the rules of the game." Bonn adds that "it is a rivalry which was incubated in acrimonious religious dispute and the struggle for life of the frontiersman." Although both

Laski's and Bonn's characterizations of the American business man are open to dispute, there is no question but that the business man plays a leading, if not the leading, role in the life of this country. As J. A. Spender observes, in paraphrasing Calvin Coolidge's famous dictum, the business of America is business, while Odette Keun asserts that this country is dominated by the business man.[28] The fact that European analysts at times criticize the American business man, therefore, does not mean that they underestimate his power and influence.

Despite the fact that such similar catastrophes as the collapse of the South Sea Bubble in 1720 have occurred at various intervals throughout European history, the American phase of the depression of 1929 has been a favorite conversation piece abroad. Although one often encounters such poor judgments as the 1928 criticism which Bernard Fay made of "the prophets of gloom" who predicted the collapse of American prosperity, this does not hinder observers abroad from dissecting the depression at length. For example, M. J. Bonn and G. D. H. Cole have detected such economically fatal combinations in the pre-depression American economy as over-production and under-spending, over-investment and under-consumption. Since American economists also have stressed these pairings, they are hardly of an original nature. As might be predicted, the economic Left does not miss the opportunity to cast brickbats at the capitalist class. Thus John Maynard Keynes states that the "financial prudence" of the great corporations hindered the recovery of this nation from the slump, while Harold Laski notes that Herbert Hoover's inability to solve the depression mirrors the failure of capitalism "to take measures against its own mistakes." Other more sympathetic thinkers shift at least part of the blame to the workings of impersonal economic laws rather than make capitalism the scapegoat.

As for the overall impact of the depression on American life, many results have been detected abroad. Widespread in its implication is the observation of Andre Maurois that "in times of crisis the individual, being menaced, seeks the protection of the herd," as a result of which "the power of the State is augmented because everyone desires protection." The ensuing movement towards collectivization in America and the advent of the New Deal are concrete proofs of the validity of this hypothesis. However, one must challenge the remark of Arnold Toynbee that the depression "unmasked" the closing of the American frontier, since an awareness of this was widespread before World War I. On the other hand, Toynbee's theory that the concept of easy money passed from the life of this nation after 1929 and the suggestion of Denis Brogan that the depression signalled the end of optimism in the United States are valid, but only for the years of the depression. It may also be true, as Harold Laski points out, that with the advent of the depression "America ceased to be the land of promise and revealed that its foundations were no different in final character from those of the old world." But such remarks are not applicable to the 1960's.

The depression of 1929 did make clear that there are certain weak spots in the American economy, and some of these will be examined now. Both Andre Maurois and Barbara Ward place considerable emphasis on the fact that a housing problem persists in the United States; they believe that many old houses should be torn down and that new ones should be built. Although almost every one would agree that such a step would be desirable, there is considerable disagreement as to whether this is to be accomplished by the government or private enterprise. Likewise, holding companies are often viewed with concern by both the economic Left and the economic Right abroad. But while Odette Keun writes that "holding companies are in any case a social danger" which "were created, apparently, to milk and exploit the underlying utility companies and the investing public," Wilhelm Ropke suggests that they be subject to "strict supervision" rather than liquidated. In addition, some observers even have criticized the prevalence of a high level of wages here. Thus Joseph Schumpeter points out that this seemingly desirable condition is often a cause of unemployment, as the fund of capital available for the payment of wages often decreases following a slump.

The speculative tendency so characteristic of American capitalism has also been attacked in Europe, especially by the socialists. Thus G. D. H. Cole is one of the more prominent critics of the American variety of speculation. As far as remedies are concerned, John Maynard Keynes suggests the lowering of high interest rates and the imposition of a transfer tax on all transactions, but it is apparent that such proposals will not gain the immediate favor of proponents of free enterprise. A suggestion which probably would find a warmer acceptance among capitalists is the recommendation of Gunnar Myrdal and Odette Keun that industry should be decentralized in the United States. Such action would give the less industrialized parts of the nation an economic boost, and it is quite evident that a move in this direction is currently being made, especially in the South.

The most debated failure of American economic life is the existence of islands of poverty in a sea of plenty. Thus J. A. Spender charges that "American industry on its present basis has no room for the incapable or half-capable," so that those who are not especially able must come off second-best economically. G. D. H. Cole similarly claims that the United States has not "banished poverty and insecurity from its people's lives," and this raises the question of whether a system in which such economic inequalities exist should be abolished in spite of its merits. It would appear that leftist European critics often adhere to this theory, although it must be admitted that the economic systems which Europe has to offer have not matched the American in performance.

A rather severe agricultural problem also exists in the United States. Although European observers have detected some progress in this field in recent years, it is probably true that this dilemma is far from being solved. Thus in speaking of the depressed condition of the agricultural classes here, Odette Keun refers to the "abject misery and the degraded hopelessness" characteristic of rural life. This assertion is doubtless an extreme one, but the census bears out the figures that Oswald Spangler cites in *The Hour of Decision* which demonstrate that the farming element is numerically on the decrease in America.[29] As for the underlying cause of this decline, Harold Laski points out that "American agriculture, by the time of the Second World War, had reached the tragic situation where its capacity to produce continually expanded while its capacity to market profitably continually declined." On the other hand, Lucien Romier and Wilhelm Ropke stress that monoculture (concentration on one crop) and over-specialization have both provided an unsound basis for the establishment of a healthy agrarian economy. In general, however, European thinkers refrain from offering comprehensive plans of agrarian reform for this country; this is one of the few areas in which they have no panaceas to offer.

Many of the remarks quoted here stress the fact that the American economy is tied to that of Europe. The English historian Geoffrey Barraclough goes so far as to claim that "the broad pattern of the postwar world, much as we may dislike it, has already been set, in part, by the inexorable development of American industrial potential between 1939 and 1945." Conversely, Gunnar Myrdal maintains that although Europe may be economically dependent on America, economic changes there and elsewhere do not always influence the United States. Both of these observations are rather extreme, but they accurately reflect the widespread European concern in regard to

American economic power. Such a concern is sometimes manifested in a rather hostile manner, as by the observation of Guglielmo Ferrero that the United States is not necessarily fitted for world leadership by virtue of its financial supremacy.[30] It must be remembered, however, that a powerful nation is invariably criticized by its weaker brethren whenever it exerts itself forcefully.

In any event, there are numerous stumbling-blocks to more harmonious trans-Atlantic relations in the economic area. For example, America is a creditor nation and Europe is a debtor continent, and this unequal relationship, as G. D. H. Cole admits, would not be solved by cancelling the war debts.[31] Likewise, the American citizenry is frequently confused by their government's practice of making both loans and grants to the countries of Europe, especially in the period since 1945. In addition, Europeans often receive American investments with resentment, and this is manifested in such expressions as "financial enslavement" and the "buying up" of Europe. Obviously the only satisfactory solution to the dilemma created by this one-sided relationship would be the attainment of a state of economic equality between Europe and the United States. There is not much likelihood that this will come about in the near future, but Europe has made noteworthy advances in recent years.

As far as the future of American capitalism is concerned, there appears to be a considerable amount of controversy abroad. Revelant here is the remark of Andre Siegfried that "the Americans once believed themselves to be economically immortal," but that now "they perceive that they are just as susceptible to death as anyone." This observation focuses attention on the fact that Americans do not have the blind faith in the capitalist system that they once had. As both Andre Maurois and Raymond Aron point out, it is quite unlikely that capitalism will survive here in totally undiluted form. Consequently, governmental intervention in the economy most likely will be a fairly common thing in the future, and the government may compete with private industry in certain fields formerly reserved to the latter.

In this connection the Tennessee Valley Authority is of special significance. While Max Beloff describes it as being empirical rather than revolutionary in character, Odette Keun labels it as "an effort . . . to adjust capitalism to the present realities." Moreover, Bertrand Russell considers the Tennessee Valley Authority to be that form of socialism which is the most likely to be adopted by a "conservative" government. It is quite probable, of course, that socialism will be introduced into the American economy in the future by means of particular socialistic projects rather than through an abrupt adoption of socialism *in toto*. For as Barbara Ward suggests, the United States "is most unlikely to make the first experiment in planned capital development," since its tradition of freedom and its record of prosperity discourage large-scale radical experimentation.

It is only fitting that an analysis of American labor be made here, for, as Joseph Schumpeter and others have pointed out, our labor movement is really not opposed to the capitalist system to the extent that it is in various other countries. Thus Arnold Toynbee observes that there has been no tendency in America for an industrial proletariat to secede from society, while one might also suggest that labor has so prospered in the United States under capitalism that it has not turned to socialism in hopes of obtaining more gains. In addition, the socialist penchant for theorizing is hostile to the American pragmatic tradition. As Raymond Bruckberger notes, Samuel Gompers had "respect *for the facts, for nature, for the test of experience*" rather than for the tenets of dogmatic radicalism. Generally speaking, then, American labor is conservative, although Odette Keun admits that she is flabbergasted by this fact.

Various points of comparison and contrast between the Old World and the New will be discussed in the fourteenth chapter, but the observations dealing with the differences between American and European labor will be examined now, since they throw additional light on the material presented here on capitalism. One dissimilarity is noted by the German economist Fritz Sternberg in his remark that the working class is less unified in the United States than it is in Europe; this lack of cohesion probably accounts for the relative lack of agitation on the part of labor here. From another point of view, Harold Laski affirms that "there is greater opportunity for the worker in America than in Europe, (and) economic mobility is greater." Considering Laski's ideological orientation, this is a most noteworthy admission. Andre Siegfried, moreover, points out that American labor relies on brains rather than brawn more than its European counterpart, and adds that labor is organized in a more complicated manner in the United States than it is in Europe. In view of these comments, one might suggest that there are certain similarities between the position of labor in the Old World and the New, but that these similarities are probably outweighed by the differences.

The failure of labor to organize politically here marks another dissimilarity between the United States and Europe. Thus the English anthropologist Geoffrey Gorer remarks that "America remains unique

among highly industrialized countries in having no political party
staffed by and representative of the trade unions." Gorer adds that
"attempts to reproduce on American soil political parties based on
the class assumptions of Europe have been ludicrous failures." This
emphasis of Gorer on the relative lack of class antagonisms in the
United States is also characteristic of the writings of many other
European observers, including Andre Siegfried. Another difficulty
that American labor faces in organizing politically is noted by Harold
Laski in his assertion that "neither of the historic parties is interested
in the trade unions except in relation to its own hold upon the
government, both in the states and in the federal sphere." Indeed,
as Laski implies, labor is not completely at home in either of the two
major political parties here. It should be remembered that the major
American political parties are fundamentally alliances seeking to gain
administrative power; hence any attempt to set up a new (labor)
party on ideological grounds would probably result in failure.

Most observers abroad are of the opinion that labor has been fairly
well treated in the United States. Admittedly, one does encounter
occasionally such indictments as the claim of Odette Keun that it
"denotes a rottenness in social affairs" when workers "should be, in
a country that boasts of its democracy, slugged, shot, gassed and
bombed by the employers, with perfect safety to the latter."[32] This
remark of Keun, however, distorts the truth, as it minimizes similar
excesses on the part of American labor. Even G. D. H. Cole admits
that American industrial relations have "about them a tang of
frontier lawlessness, and of lynch law," and few objective observers
would deny that labor as well as capital has at times been ruthless
in its behavior here.

One might dismiss as an example of anti-labor extremism the quite
dissimilar assertion of Ludwig von Mises that the American laborer
tends to underestimate what Big Business has done for him. Yet it
must be admitted that quite a few European commentators of a more
moderate turn of mind have been puzzled by the charge that labor is
being persecuted here. This theory is quite difficult to reconcile with
the fact that labor enjoys more tangible benefits in this nation than
it does anywhere else in the world. In addition, labor in the U. S. has
its faults. Even Harold Laski admits that the American labor czar
is often a benevolent despot and that our trade unions frequently
behaves too much as pressure groups and not enough as model
democracies. It seems illogical, therefore, that the left-wing element
abroad would picture the American capitalist as a scapegoat and the

American laborer as a martyr. Fortunately, the trend at the moment is in the direction of more realistic appraisals, although one still encounters odious distortions.

For numerous reasons, it is extremely difficult to formulate a set of conclusions relating to American capitalism and labor which would be generally accepted abroad (or at home). Even the fact that the laborer enjoys a higher standard of living under the capitalist system here than does his European counterpart is brushed aside by many foreign critics. This is because the latter often claim that the working class in the United States has been exposed to severe depressions resulting from the excesses of capitalism. Similarly, the fact that American labor has been strong enough politically to be the deciding factor in many state and national elections does not impress the more hostile European commentators. The latter generally charge that American capitalists constantly harass labor by supporting such measures as right-to-work laws which would reduce the political power of the unions. But regardless of the endless arguments pro and con, an examination of American history proves that both capital and labor have prospered under the American system of free enterprise, while both socialism and communism have attracted few followers in this nation. The following chapter will examine the record of radicalism in the United States, and as this chapter is a chronicle of victory, the next one will be a journal of defeat.

CHAPTER VII

RADICALISM AND RUSSIA

Karl Marx once expressed the opinion that the world revolution would break out first in those nations with the most highly developed industrial economies. But time has thus far proved him wrong. The United States, in fact, is the prize exhibit in the gallery of advanced capitalist countries which have refrained from embracing the Marxian ideology.

Despite the fact that, as Luigi Barzini observes, "the United States is a nation founded in the rebellion against the ancient order," American history has been characterized by a stability and order which is the very antithesis of the revolutionary spirit. Thus Denis Brogan asserts that "the idea of a conscious rebuilding of society on a basis of common ownership is still un-American," while Raoul de Roussy de Sales expresses the belief that "the American people are more conservative than any other." Both opinions reflect the non-revolutionary assessment of American life that is common among European thinkers.

The quite noticeable lack of success of socialism in the United States may be attributed to many factors. One is that the economic opportunities which the capitalist system offers to the masses act as a brake against socialism. Another is that up to 1890 the frontier functioned as an outlet for tensions which might otherwise have been discharged through socialist experimentation. In regard to the former, Bernard Fay asserts that immigrants were attracted to America because they wanted to be proprietors and capitalists rather than because they were interested in spreading radical ideas. This thesis largely explains why the proletariat did not serve as a catalyst in the abortive attempt of a few intellectuals to institute socialism here. On the other hand, one might regard as rather curious Fay's remark that such a left-wing ideology is "for the most part an offshoot of worldliness or the result of sexual troubles." The absence of revolutionary feeling within the American proletariat is also stressed by Arnold Toynbee, who speaks of the masses still being under the influence of the "dream of the golden nineteenth-century opportunities which are actually no longer open to them.'" But Toynbee does not offer any evidence to substantiate his belief that the proletariat will soon lose its docility.

In regard to the frontier as a damper on the growth of American socialism, Wilhelm Ropke notes that the presence of free land hindered the development of an industrial proletariat. Ropke adds, however, that since the closing of the frontier conditions in the United States have become more and more like those in Europe. Quite obviously some of the energy that formerly went into pioneering was diverted into production after 1890, but this obviously is no proof that a modification of the economic system accompanied this change (as Ropke claims). Thus G. D. H. Cole maintains that the cause of socialism was not aided by the closing of the frontier. Cole attributes the socialists' lack of success to the fact that the American masses are not as politically minded as their European brethren, as well as to the split in the American working class between the privileged and unprivileged elements. These observations by Cole are substantiated by the history of the American labor movement, although they do not explain by themselves the poor record of American socialism.

European thinkers have offered various other theories for the relative failure of the American socialist movement. One rather important hypothesis is the one of M. J. Bonn that "the theory of Socialism, especially of the Marxist brand, did not attract Americans (because) it was too abstract." It is a common belief among foreign thinkers that American thought, unlike European, is essentially pragmatic rather than abstract, and thus it is to be expected that a highly developed ideological system would not be very palatable to the American taste. Another interesting explanation is set forth by Raymond Aron, who attributes the weak impact of socialism to the fact that the proletariat here is composed of a "multiplicity of nationalities." For this reason, it is more difficult for the proletariat to unite in a common cause than it would be if it were homogenous. Still another suggestion is offered by Joseph Schumpeter, who points out that the agrarian element in the United States has generally been opposed to the development of socialism. This theory is a quite logical one, as the farmer and the socialist hold different concepts of the ultimate source of wealth, and this and other factors have prevented them from working together in harmony.

Although the socialists have not imposed their ideology on American life, one might logically expect that they would have had more success in assaulting the bastions of organized labor, but such has not been the case. Even such a confirmed socialist as Harold Laski admits that "a successful trade-union leader in the United States has far more of the habit and outlook of a prosperous business executive there than he has of the outlook of a trade-union leader in Europe." Laski's observation is substantiated by the fact that one does not encounter the hostility between labor and capital in this country that one does in Europe. In addition, American socialists have made few first-rate contributions to the body of world socialist theory, and G. D. H. Cole even claims in his monumental *History of Socialistic Thought* that to date there has been no American writer of this persuasion of any real consequence. Of course, many European thinkers have recognized the importance of Henry George,[33] but George actually was a quasi-Physiocrat (land rather than labor is the ultimate source of value) and thus does not fit into the main line of developing socialist dogma. This lack of distinguished American socialist theorists, taken in conjunction with the failure of socialists to influence American labor in a noticeable manner, provides final proof that the record of socialism in the United States has been a dismal one.

The chances of socialism playing a more important role in American economic life in the future are generally regarded as greater than its relative failure in the past would indicate. Even Joseph Schumpeter, a staunch friend of capitalism, predicts that the socialist system will eventually replace the capitalist one in the United States. Ludwig von Mises similarly expresses doubt as to the future of capitalism here, and he writes that "the main issue in present-day political struggles is whether society should be organized on the basis of private ownership of the means of production ... or on the basis of public control." Of course, it was pointed out in the last chapter that it is conceivable that certain features of socialism may become part of the American economy without it being accepted in its entirety. This is reflected in Jacques Maritain's prophecy that an economic system will evolve in the United States which will be neither capitalist nor socialist in nature. But as far as socialists themselves are concerned, they are not especially optimistic about the future of their ideas in the United States. Most of them probably would agree with G. D. H. Cole that it would take another depression to deal a death blow to capitalism here.

Unimpressive as the record of socialism in the United States may be, it is not even approached by that of communism. The above analysis of the failure of the socialist movement here is also largely applicable to the communist one. In addition, it must be remembered that communism is an essentially revolutionary ideology, and thus fits into the American way of life even less than does socialism. One might note in this connection the perceptive remark of Denis de Rougemont that those nations in which the Reformation had the greatest impact (among which he lists the United States) are also the ones in which communism has made the least headway, mainly because the Reformation itself embodied numerous revolutionary ideals which eventually become a part of their historical tradition. Nevertheless, it is generally agreed that communists have had some slight success in recruiting new members here since 1929, although their membership probably had begun to decline by the time that the late Senator Joseph McCarthy began his crusade.

In writing of the communist membership drive of the last generation, Denis Brogan asserts that this movement is a result of the impact of the depression of 1929 on American life, although this theory does not explain the presence of communism here among members of the upper class of society. On the other hand, Ludwig von Mises and many other European critics have often noted that Marxism attracts show business people, and Norman Angell has uncovered communist influences even in such an unlikely place as among the American isolationists. While the claim of Angell is perhaps fanciful, there is considerably more justification for the accusation of Von Mises, especially as it pertains to the decade of the 1940's. In any event, most Americans are perplexed by the fact that some of their brethren are attracted by Marxism, and the anti-commuist often has difficulty in explaining this phenomenon to them.

As for history in general, Raymond Aron observes that "there is no country in which it is impossible to organize at least a minor Communist movement." Aron adds that since communism in its initial stages is a conspiracy rather than a mass phenomenon, one encounters it in this form in the United States. Admittedly Oswald Spengler has observed that a "progressive Bolshevization of the masses" has been taking place in this nation. But if America is tending towards a classless society, as Andre Maurois also suggests, it will probably be within the framework of a modified capitalist system rather than within that of a more radical ideology.

Actually pure communism probably has a limited appeal even to the small coterie of radical intellectuals who are opposed to capitalism. Thus Rom Landau suggests with considerable justification that "pro-Communist attitudes and sentiments (in the United States) are the direct outcome of pressure at the hands of the reactionary elements." In fact, those liberals who defend various communists whom they believe to have been "persecuted" usually do so because they feel that the right of freedom of speech is being threatened, not because they are in sympathy with communism. Few are the doctrinal ties between American liberalism and Russian Marxism.

The growing awareness that communism is a threat to the American way of life did not, of course, begin with Senator McCarthy. This fact actually had become clear to many observers as long as five years before McCarthy began his anti-communist activities. In addition, there has always been a small hard core of Bolshevik baiters in this country since the outbreak of the 1917 Revolution in Russia. But while most European thinkers are anti-communist, this does not deter them from taking a dim view of many of the forms that the anti-communist crusade has assumed here. It should be kept in mind, however, that an examination of their writings before 1950 (and even later) reveals that more than one commentator abroad has not been as vigilant as he should have been. Thus Arnold Toynbee asserts in a 1947 article that the present Western fear of communism is not based on the probability of Russian military aggression, but rather that "the Communist weapon that is making America so jumpy . . . is the spiritual engine of propaganda." In lieu of such bad judgments as this one, it is not surprising that many European writers are quite sensitive on the subject of communism, and this touchiness is often manifested in their writings.

A typical expression of the "McCarthyphobia" so prevalent among both American and European liberals is the observation of Simone de Beauvoir that during the era of McCarthy "everyone of the Left was accused of being a Communist, and every Communist was a traitor." Harold Laski similarly maintains that "anti-Communist activity endangers the freedom of every official, every teacher, and the overwhelming majority of clergy, in the United States." Laski also claims that the anti-Communist "hysteria" which reached its peak between 1950 and 1954 in this nation adversely affected the rate of Soviet democratization. An example of even more confused thinking is Norman Angell's declaration that "the true function of American policy is to build up power, not against Communism, but against aggression." One may agree with Geoffrey Gorer that apathy and passivity are more of a threat to American democracy than socialism or communism, but this is no reason to ignore the danger that Marxism poses to the safety of the United States. It does seem, moreover, that the tendency abroad is at times to underestimate rather than to overestimate the communist menace.

The role of fascism in American history also has been of interest to European thinkers, but it has received far less attention than that of socialism and communism. Yet Odette Keun and other European liberals often maintain that if America is ever to fall victim to an extremist philosophy, it will be one of the fascist variety,[34] and they usually regard Huey Long as the type of individual who would lead such a movement here. It is also a favorite theme with Harold Laski and other left-wing observers abroad that big business in the United states manifests certain fascist tendencies. This belief is predicated on the reasoning that since many American business men are not vitally interested in widespread social and economic reforms, they are therefore proponents of a reactionary philosophy. But most authorities recognize that the general political and economic trend in this country at the moment is slightly towards the left; as of late 1961 there does not appear to be much chance of the radical right taking over the control of the United States in the near future, regardless of the complaints and warnings of the Keuns and the Laskis.

As far as the international aspects of radicalism are concerned one might cite various ties between radical groups in the Old World and the New. For example, Frank Thistlethwaite places considerable emphasis on the cordial relationship which existed between British and American radicals during the early Nineteenth Century. The radical element, however, has constituted only a very small proportion of the population at any time in American history. Moreover, whatever attraction the United States may have offered at one time to the European revolutionary element had by the mid-Twentieth Century largely disappeared, as Bertrand Russell points out. It must be remembered, however, that this decline of America as the promised land of radicalism has been paralleled by the rise of a new Jerusalem in Moscow. Regardless of the old saying that the more things change the more they are the same, a century ago Russia was the land of the past and America the country of the future, while today the roles are reversed. (Or at least so the communists think.) Therefore, an examination of the relationship which exists between the United States and the Soviet Union provides a fitting conclusion to this study of radicalism.

There are many aspects to the current struggle between America and Russia, and European observers have commented at length on most of them. The stereotyped view abroad that international tensions will continue for an indefinite period is reflected in the remark of G. D. H. Cole that "there would seem to be no answer, short of war, except that the world will have to be divided into two spheres of influence, with the one system in operation in the one sphere, and the other in the other." Likewise, Raymond Aron is representative of European thought in that he suggests that the position of this country is superior to that of its Marxian rival in regard to personal rights, freedom of self-expression and criticism, and the economic benefits that the masses enjoy.

In addition, there is in Europe a widespread disbelief that an either-or choice must be made between the United States and the Soviet Union. Thus Arnold Toynbee complains of the propaganda coming from both countries that "in the mouths of these loud-speakers one does not hear the still small voice." This lament is obviously correlated with Toynbee's conviction that both democracy and communism are Christian heresies. Raymond Aron reflects another common European sentiment in his remark that America is more interested in converting the world to democracy than it is in providing for its own safety, and that this crusading zeal increases the danger of an ideological war between this country and Russia. Europeans invariably feel that such a war is not neccessary, and for this reason they attempt to eliminate ideological tensions, as they fear that these would be the factor most likely to detonate an explosion.

Most European writers, however, are inclined to believe that the differences between America and Russia will be settled in some peaceful manner, and they usually cite the horrors of nuclear warfare as the main deterrent to possible armed strife. On the other hand, if there is a full-scale holocaust, there is little doubt but that it will be the most destructive one in the history of humanity. Thus Sidney and Beatrice Webb observe that "the class war, if and when battle is joined in earnest, will be one of the wars of religion, and may be waged on a scale and with a ferocity, a self-sacrifice, and a persistence which will make the religious wars of the seventeenth century seem mere riots by comparison."

But the Webbs' fear is not universally shared by their colleagues. Fritz Sternberg has pointed out that pronounced ideological differences have not resulted in a war between America and Russia in the past, and that this provides a basis for assuming that no world-wide conflict will break out in the future.[35] Sternberg even suggests that the tensions present in the world today should not be wholly attributed to the struggle between the democratic and communist ways of life. Indeed, it is quite possible that the growing nationalist movement in former colonial areas may take the edge off the current struggle between the United States and the Soviet Union.

It is noteworthy that European observers often detect various similarities between America and Russia. In addition, they frequently contrast these two nations with Europe instead of emphasizing the schism which exists between the United States and the Soviet Union. Denis de Rougemont, for example, asserts that the "heresies of Progress" have displayed their full effects in the United States and the Soviet Union rather than in Europe.[36] The fact that so many European thinkers compare rather than contrast America and Russia is significant, as it may reflect their hope that the differences between the two countries may not be great enough to lead to war.

In summarizing some of the similarities, Oswald Spengler observes that America and Russia resemble each other in their breadth of landscape, economic basis of society, and standardization of life. One might also cite in this connection Luigi Barzini's reference to a common propagandizing attitude as to ideology and principle, and Bertrand Russell's mention of a mutual belief in the energies of man and the exploitation of nature. Similarly of consequence is Wyndham Lewis' allusion to the exaggerated emphasis on mass life typical of both nations. It is, in fact, quite significant that European observers compare America and Russia on so many different points. Moreover, those critics who contrast these two countries, despite their vociferousness, generally confine themselves to chronicling a handful of differences, particularly those which Raymond Aron points out a few pages back.

Even from the economic point of view there is a widespread belief abroad that the United States and the Soviet Union are not irreconcilable opposites. Thus Arnold Toynbee observes that "if man were nothing more than economic man, there would be no reason in the world why Russia and America should collide with one another for generations to come." Toynbee maintains in this connection that the main issue at stake between these two nations is moral rather than economic. On the other hand, G. D. H. Cole, in writing of the impact of "Americanism" on the Russian economy, theorizes that the essential difference between the two countries is political.[37] It should be noted, however, that Cole emphasizes the general importance of the economic factor in history more so than does Toynbee.

As far as specific economic similarities are concerned, Joseph Schumpeter makes a noteworthy comparison between the redistribution of wealth carried out in modern America with that effected in Russia since 1917. It is, moreover, true that the attempt of the New Deal to modify the distribution of income in the United States does bear

some similarity to related Soviet experiments. Other points of comparison, such as the existence of a privileged economic class and a
high rate of industrialization, might also be mentioned. In addition,
it must be remembered that those thinkers (both here and abroad)
who emphasize the economic contrast between the United States
and the Soviet Union generally do not make their observations on
the basis of a complete economic study. This is because they usually
confine themselves to an examination of the question of who controls the instruments of production, while ignoring other aspects of
the economic situation.

It might be added in this connection that Europeans often make
remarks contrasting America and Russia which are of questionable
validity. Thus Arnold Toynbee observes that "the Russian people's
habitual and characteristic temper was one of docile resignation, the
American people's one of obstreperous impatience." Toynbee's statement must be challenged because blood-letting has been far more
prevalent in Russian than in American history. On the other hand,
Hermann von Keyserling writes that the American soul is expressed in
the "language of prosperity" and the Bolshevik soul in the "language of
poverty." One might suggest here that if economic conditions in
Russia are sub-par, this is partly a fault of the tsarist regime, and
should not be blamed entirely on the communists. As a final example,
Bernard Fay's observations on the American and communist world
views illustrate how even a prominent historian may establish a faulty
contrast. While Fay is perhaps correct in labelling the Marxian dogma
as "a great dream, youthful and optimistic," he errs badly in his claim
that American civilization is built on "a foundation of sage pessimism
and renunciation." Of course, those commentators who compare the
United States and the Soviet Union are not always correct, and those
who contrast them are not always wrong, but one does obtain the
impression that the former often are more accurate than the latter.

In relating these remarks comparing America and Russia to the
material presented in the first part of this chapter, one is struck
by a seeming paradox. Many European critics apparently regard
that nation in which left-wing ideologies have met their most noteworthy rebuff as quite similar to that country which is today perhaps
the ultimate embodiment of radicalism. If one is to explain this paradox, he must harmonize the theory that the similarities between the
United States and the Soviet Union are trivial with the one that these
two countries are not the ideological opposites which they are often regarded abroad as being. In an era in which the spokesmen of each

nation invariably represent the contrast between America and Russia in black and white terms, it is indeed difficult to accept the possibility that the truth may actually be gray. But it must be admitted that the theory that these two countries must be either totally alike or completely different manifests a mathematical necessity which is obviously out of place in historical analysis. Moreover, any truly perceptive investigation of the rapport or lack thereof between the United States and the Soviet Union reveals that the old familiar stereotypes are often a hindrance rather than a help.

CHAPTER VIII

THE DILEMMA OF THE NEW DEAL

The significance of the New Deal and the greatness of Franklin Roosevelt are among the most widely debated issues of recent years. To some social scientists the New Deal preserved that which was worth saving in capitalism, while to others it marked the death knell for that economic system. Likewise, F.D.R. has been characterized by various commentators both as one of the great figures of this era and as one of the leading civilization-wreckers of the age. Since Americans have considerable difficulty in obtaining the proper perspective from which to make an objective judgment on either F.D.R. or the New Deal, evaluations from a more detached point of view are indeed welcome.

Europeans have compared Franklin D. Roosevelt to a wider variety of historical figures than any other American of the twentieth century; many of the parallels which have been drawn are quite striking. Thus H. G. Wells pairs F. D. R. and Joseph Stalin as men who "were attempting to produce a huge, modern, scientifically organized, socialist state, the one out of a warning crisis and the other out of a chaos." Wells' analogy is a typical representation of Roosevelt as an extreme leftwinger. Another striking parallel is that set forth by the English socialist politician and writer R. H. S. Crossman, who asserts that F. D. R.'s counterpart in British politics is the late nineteenth century statesman Joseph Chamberlain. Crossman also hypothesizes that "it is idle to argue whether he (Roosevelt) was a Conservative who saved capitalism or a Liberal who transformed it." It must be remembered in this connection that Chamberlain was a Liberal in his early days in British politics; he became a Conservative later when he felt that a change was politically expedient.

As American equivalents of F. D. R., Harold Laski suggests Theodore Roosevelt and Woodrow Wilson, although Laski qualifies his comparison with the remark that F. D. R. was more successful than were his two predecessors. This parallel has also been drawn by American historians. What is significant about these analogies is that they are all the conceptions of contemporary British socialists, yet Franklin Roosevelt has been variously pictured as a socialist, as a person to

79

whom no label should be applied, and as a liberal. When three educated men of a similar ideological bent arrive at such diverse evaluations of an individual, it is to be expected that a more varied group of thinkers would come no closer to agreement.

Although a number of commentators label Franklin Roosevelt as either a conservative or a liberal, European thinkers often regard him as a man without a set philosophical doctrine. This belief has led to his placement in a rather wide variety of categories. Thus Andre Sieg-fried, no admirer of the economic policies of Franklin Roosevelt, considers him "a pure opportunist, and probably an essentially light-hearted man." On the other hand, Amaury de Riencourt regards F. D. R. as a pragmatist, while Harold Laski speaks of Franklin Roosevelt's "experimental temper."[38] A cynic might observe that an opportunist is a pragmatist or experimentalist who adopts policies with which the person doing the labelling disagrees. It is, of course, true that flexibility may be both a vice and a virtue. But F.D.R. is con-demned by some Europeans because he was a socialist or a communist (which would necessitate an adherence to a particular set of beliefs), as well as criticized by others because he failed to provide a definite program of reform based on some systematic ideology. Thus, as was the case with Woodrow Wilson and his foreign policy, the founder of the New Deal has been the victim of adverse characterizations which are somewhat inconsistent with each other.

Many psychologically minded individuals have gone to great lengths to determine wherein the secret of Franklin Roosevelt's personal magnetism lay. The answer probably rests in a combination of recep-tivity and communicativeness, both of which qualities often have been noted by European critics. Thus Wyndham Lewis writes that F. D. R.'s receptive frame of mind compensated for whatever he lacked in ability, while Odette Keun observes that he had the facility to com-municate the aspirations of the common man. Andre Siegfried sums up both qualities succinctly in his remark that "one has the impression, when he speaks to him, that he is addressing a human being, who un-derstands you and who wishes to assist you." Siegfried's observation throws light on the identification that Franklin Roosevelt was able to create between the common man and himself, which rapport was largely responsible for his success.

In the final pages of *War and Peace* Leo Tolstoy sets forth the thesis that great men are the result of events, rather than vice versa. It would appear that Franklin Roosevelt appeared on the national scene at the moment most favorable for him to seize power. On the other hand, few European writers have gone so far as to assert that F. D. R. was merely a passive reed in a strong gale; more frequent is the charge that he exerted a dictatorial authority in making use of the powers of his office.

It is beyond question that a crisis existed when Franklin Roosevelt assumed the Presidency. Thus Harold Laski observes that had F. D. R. embraced the "gospel of Coolidge and Hoover . . . it is difficult to see how America could have passed through the nine months (of 1933) without a major drift towards a revolutionary condition." Laski adds that "the failure of Mr. Roosevelt meant the end of political democracy in America." Denis Brogan similarly writes that had the Republicans retained control of the government they would also have been forced to enact measures of a rather drastic type; even some Republicans subscribe to this theory today.

The term New Deal implies a break with the past, but the Roose-veltian reforms were really a highly complex phenomenon composed of diverse elements, some very modern, others quite old. Bernard Fay observes of the New Deal that "the President and the people of the United States have proved that they were able to discard the past entirely" but this judgment appears to be an extreme one. A more moderate appraisal is that of Arnold Toynbee, who visualizes the New Deal as an "attempt at comprehensive and systematic regula-tion of private economic life." The opinion that the Rooseveltian reforms were revolutionary is also expressed by Ludwig von Mises, a conservative economist who holds that the New Deal was the first step in the establishment of communism in the United States. This belief, be it noted, is based on the assumption that any form of govern-mental control of private life is a mere prelude to progressive inter-vention in this sphere, and this conclusion is not necessarily valid.

Certain other European thinkers are not so willing to recognize the uniqueness of the New Deal. Thus Odette Keun remarks that "the reforms that seemed so startling to the American people are in Europe merely subjects of academic discussion," while Denis Brogan avers that "the New Deal was basically, in intention and effect, conserva-tive." Writers of this persuasion invariably set forth a long list of re-forms enacted prior to 1933 in both the United States and Europe, placing special emphasis on measures instituted by Lloyd George, Theodore Roosevelt, and Woodrow Wilson. Some European thinkers even have been imaginative enough to trace the Rooseveltian policies back to ancient Rome. Thus Bertrand de Jouvenel and Amaury de Riencourt have compared the legislation of F. D. R. with that of

certain early Roman emperors. It is not surprising, therefore, that
many of the critics of the New Deal have labelled the Rooseveltian
program as reactionary rather than as radical and that they have frequently pictured Franklin Roosevelt as a mock liberal rather than a
great innovator.

Indecision over the exact nature of the New Deal is characteristic of
the observations of Harold Laski, one of the closest students of the
Rooseveltian reforms. An examination of Laski's views provides added evidence that about the only generalization which one may accurately make about the New Deal is that no generalization is valid.
Admittedly those of his statements that tend to uphold the thesis that
the Rooseveltian reforms were unique appear to be quite uncompromising. Thus Laski remarks that "President Roosevelt is the first
statesman in a great capitalist society who has sought deliberately and
systematically to use the power of the state to subordinate the primary
assumpions of that society to certain vital social purposes."   But
Laski also asserts that F. D. R. "was never convinced that the foundations of the Americanism he inherited were really inadequate to the
demands made upon its institutional expression." When one encounters such diverse evaluations from the same author, it is hardly surprising that the leading thinkers of Europe characterize the New Deal
in so many different ways.

A possible means of reconciling the wide variety of observations on
the Rooseveltian reforms lies in Laski's statement that "what in the
New Deal is new in the treatment of them"—i.e., such problems as the
evils of monopoly, monetary instability, etc—"is less the manner
than the continuity and the persistence with which they have been
attacked." Laski here emphasizes the form that the Rooseveltian
reforms took rather than their actual content as the key to their
originality. This evaluation has a parallel in the field of art or music,
where a creator of genius will take certain stylistic ideas of his predecessors and fuse them into an original painting or composition.
Keeping this analogy in mind, Laski's reference to the New Deal as a
modernized version of Jeffersonian democracy gains in significance.
One might suggest that F. D. R. used the traditions of the past as a
basis on which to build a new edifice, and thus conclude that he was
an evolutionist rather than a revolutionist.

The parallel which Laski draws between Lloyd George and Franklin
Roosevelt is also of interest in that the English reforms of the early
twentieth century provided a background in which the developing
Laski formulated his ideas on social change. Thus Laski observes of

the New Deal that "most of its measures were of the type that we
associate with the Liberal government of 1906-14 in Britain" and that
"the adventure upon which Mr. Roosevelt embarked last March is
not a new one in history." But here Laski seems to confuse that
distinction which he makes elsewhere between form and content;
his interjection of English history into his analysis of the New Deal
results in confusion rather than clarification.

A question related to the one of whether the New Deal was systematic is that of whether the Rooseveltian reforms really established a
planned economy in America. Despite the protestations of such conservative European thinkers as Ludwig von Mises, there appears to be
considerable agreement that the New Deal was somewhat makeshift
in character, whatever its philosophical base. Thus G. D. H. Cole
notes that "the Roosevelt economy could work only as long as the
American public were prepared to stand for a continuous piling up of
the National Debt." Cole also contends that neither the Rooseveltian
reforms nor "Nazi work-finding" were feasible as permanent solutions to the problems facing the economies of America and Germany.
It is noteworthy that Cole here denies on utilitarian grounds the possibility of the New Deal being a long range attempt at the reorganization of society; this logic reflects the typically socialist view that
capitalism has now reached the point where it is beyond salvation.

Fritz Sternberg, who is also a socialist, similarly argues that *"this
extension of the State sector* (by F. D. R.) *was never intended to be
permanent,"* and that Roosevelt had "no systematic plan to combat
the crisis" (the depression of 1929). But Sternberg does not present as
strong a case for his ideas as does Cole. The German economist
obviously is of the opinion that behind every plan of action there must
be a set philosophical doctrine; New Deal planning, in his eyes,
lacks this ideological characteristic or orientation. Sternberg's observations (as well as those of Cole) are important in that they illustrate
how such concrete terms as planning and regulation have lost their
sharpness in the increasingly complex world of today. If it is incorrect
to regard the New Deal as mere planning, it is also wrong to describe it
as simply a series of regulations. Thus one is confronted with a twilight
zone in which it is extremely difficult to apply the labels so readily
bantered around in former days.

In regard to specific criticisms of the New Deal, it is noteworthy that
Franklin Roosevelt's currency reforms have been widely attacked
by both the right and left wings of the European politico-economic
spectrum. Even Harold Laski, whom no one would regard as a critic

of F. D. R., does not hesitate to throw a few brickbats at his currency measures. Laski charges, for example, that Roosevelt at times supported the idea of the compensated dollar and at other times opposed this concept. Monetary stability always has been an important consideration to European economists, especially those of the classical school. For this reason, it is not surprising that Europeans would be less tolerant of the experimental maneuverings of F. D. R. in the monetary sphere than elsewhere.

Wilhelm Ropke, the ideological antithesis of Laski, similarly attacks the abandonment of the gold standard by the Roosevelt administration "as one of the most disastrous acts on record of any government and any country in recent times." Ropke is also somewhat disenchanted with certain other New Deal actions, such as the devaluation of the dollar. It must be remembered, of course, that many of the economic measures enacted during this period had the fundamental objective of helping the American economy first and the world economy second. Consequently, F.D.R.'s failure to support the London Economic Conference of 1933 was widely criticized abroad. Although Bernard Fay maintains that this conference would not have achieved much anyway, a considerable number of European observers believe that his action dealt a death blow to the international gold standard. Many, in fact, have never forgiven Franklin Roosevelt for "sabotaging" this meeting.

In view of the chronic farm problem existing in the United States, it is perhaps surprising that the Rooseveltian reforms in the agricultural field have been praised. Such is the case, although much of the applause came from European leftists. Thus Odette Keun writes that "it is in the field of agriculture that I was most impressed by the 'newness' of the New Deal methods." John Maynard Keynes similarly lauds the crop reduction scheme contained in the first Agricultural Adjustment Act (1933); he notes that "the reduction of (agricultural) stocks to a normal level was a necessary process—a phase which had to be endured." It is ironical that both Keun and Keynes applaud the rescuing of the American farmer from his own productive fertility, as the problem in Europe is generally one of increasing the agricultural output rather than limiting it. The differing agrarian difficulties of the Old World and the New explains in part why, as was pointed out in the sixth chapter, European critics rarely propose comprehensive programs of reform to the American farmer.

Apart from its immediate ramifications, the effect of the New Deal on American history has been a continuing one. Andre Siegfried even claims that the Rooseveltian program of reform in combination with the depression of 1929 has been the most significant historical phenomenon in American life since the Declaration of Independence. Siegfried also observes that when F.D.R. assumed the Presidency, "the Democratic Party relinquished its traditions and became the champion of federal control, the upholder of trade unionism, and above all, the dispenser of social benefits." This point was brought out previously in the fourth chapter. Harold Laski, on the other hand, speaks of the growth of a "sense of state" in America during the Roosevelt Administration. Laski notes in addition that the national government has come to assume a more important role in the life of the American people. Both of Laski's observations reflect the almost universal agreement among European thinkers that the New Deal has been a major force in modern American life, especially in the fields of politics and government. This has been the judgment of both his admirers and crities.

Speaking of the more cosmic implications of the New Deal, Bertrand de Jouvenel observes that F. D. R. was the embodiment of the "securitarian aspirations of our time." This is a noteworthy remark, as his critics have often charged that Franklin Roosevelt instituted policies which exchanged liberty for security. But this movement towards security is, as de Jouvenel points out, world-wide in scope rather than confined to the United States. In this connection reference should be made to the observation of Raoul de Roussy de Sales that "the Four Freedoms program of Roosevelt thus appears as a bridge linking, in a plausible formula, the inheritance of the past and the hopes of the future." Actually those freedoms which F. D. R. advocated may be divided into two pairs, one consisting of freedom of speech and ownership, the other of freedom from want and war. Such a division reflects both the libertarian aspirations of the past and the securitarian hopes of the years ahead. But as a new era was ushered in by the inauguration of F. D. R., an old one was also ushered out. Thus Philip Guedalla notes that the coming of the New Deal marked the decline in power of the wealthy "robber barons," whose careers were "the American equivalent of drum-and-trumpet history in the Old World." Guedalla also remarks that the continuance of such men in positions of power would have led to fascism rather than democracy, and this is a theory which apologists for the New Deal have often proposed.

But the fact that the Rooseveltian reforms were of prime significance in American history does not imply as a corollary that the New Deal as a whole was desirable. In fact, many conservatively minded European critics regard the policies of F. D. R. as a curse rather than a blessing. Thus Wilhelm Ropke observes that the wave of "group egotism" which accompanied the Rooseveltian reforms was a symptom of regression rather than progress, and he also maintains that the Roosevelt Administration supplied aid to those groups controlling the most votes rather than to those who most needed assistance. Ropke here manifests a distrust of the masses which is highly suspect in liberal circles, but he raises an important point in his charge that F. D. R. often geared his reforms to political expediency.

Andre Siegfried, on the other hand, refers to the "spendthrift demagogy" of the Roosevelt Administration, while Andre Maurois charges that Franklin Roosevelt succeeded rather imperfectly in putting the economy back in operation. These observations are typical expressions of the belief that the New Deal was not successful in executing its economic policies, as many critics of F. D. R. refuse to discern a cause and effect relationship between the New Deal program and this nation's recovery from the depression. A large number of the criticisms of the New Deal are, of course, founded on the assumption that governmental action is essentially undesirable. Wilhelm Ropke, for example, writes that "as long as we do not take the foolhardy plunge into the total Office or Command Economy, all measures of Planning are liable only to hinder recovery." This and similar remarks provides conclusive evidence that the proponents of *laissez-faire* have as yet to admit defeat.

Quite obviously European commentators would not show such interest in the New Deal were it not for the fact that they regard the Rooseveltian reforms as being of significance for Europe as well as America. Noteworthy in this regard is Harold Laski's 1933 remark that "Europe has caught something of the sense of exhilaration which has attended Mr. Roosevelt's accession to office." Many European liberals, of course, felt at this time that F. D. R. was preparing to establish a new order in the United States. Laski also asserts it is difficult to conceive of how Franklin Roosevelt could solve the problems facing America without reference to Europe, although F. D. R. more or less attempted to do so during the first year or more of his administration. Moreover, Laski maintains that a program of debt settlement, tariff reduction, and currency stablization would be of benefit to the European economy. As history reveals, the second of these points was handled most to the liking of Europeans, while the first was more or less settled by default, and the latter is still a matter of controversy. Although the actions of Franklin Roosevelt as President perhaps did not fulfill the expectations of the more revolutionary minded Europeans, most liberals abroad do feel that F. D. R. exerted a positive force on American life and set an example for the Old World to follow.

In short, over the last quarter century Franklin Roosevelt and the New Deal have been widely discussed on the other side of the Atlantic. However, Europeans commentators are no more in agreement on these two topics than are their American counterparts, and this lack of consensus may be attributed to various factors. One thorny problem that one encounters in attempting to pass judgment on F. D. R's program of reform is that the concept of liberalism has undergone an evolution in recent years. Moreover, the pragmatic aspect of the New Deal is a complicating element, as pragmatism cuts across the old dividing line between conservatism and liberalism. Other stumbling-blocks might also be mentioned, such as the difficulty in drawing meaningful correlations between American and European politics, and in conjunction these make the task of evaluation formidable.

As a result, one hesitates to offer any set of conclusions on the domestic program of Franklin Roosevelt other than to make the cautious suggestion that it was a step in the direction of centralizing power in the hands of the national government. Twenty-five years is a relatively short period in which to pass judgment on any historical phenomenon; it is both difficult and unreasonable to place the New Deal in its proper historical perspective in terms of so limited a span of time. Moreover, the political philosophy prevailing at some future date may be quite at variance with that in vogue now, and Franklin Roosevelt and his program of domestic reform thus may appear in a quite different perspective then than they now do. On the other hand, F. D. R.'s international policies generally have met with approval abroad (despite widespread criticisms at home), but an analysis of this subject must be postponed until the tenth chapter.

Chapter IX

IMPERIALISM VERSUS ISOLATIONISM

The foreign relations of the United States are that aspect of American life which is probably of the most interest to European observers. The presence, however, of several seemingly irreconcilable elements in the attitude of this nation towards the remainder of the world complicates matters somewhat. Although one might list quite a few trends in the evolution of American foreign policy, three main elements stand out: imperialism, isolationism, and internationalism. The imperialist impulse is of a dualistic nature in that a distinction might be made between continental and overseas expansion. The same thing is also true of the isolationist element; there exists an essential difference between its role in American life before and after this country became a world power around the turn of the century. These two topics are dealt with in the present chapter; internationalism is analyzed in the chapter that follows.

In discussing the continental expansion phase of American imperialism, Frank Thistlethwaite describes Manifest Destiny as a "programme of westward territorial aggrandizement."[39] In general, the only aspect of American foreign policy prior to 1898 which is regarded abroad as markedly imperialist is the Mexican War. This is because Europeans deem to be of minor importance such features of nineteenth century American diplomacy as the Ostend Manifesto of 1854 on the annexation of Cuba, and the attempt of the Grant Administration to place the Dominican Republic under the American flag. Despite the protests of the Ruben Darios and Manuel Ugartes south of the border, the Monroe Doctrine is considered to be the cornerstone of American isolationism rather than that of American imperialism. About the only exception that one might make to this rule is an 1848 proclamation by President Polk which invoked the Monroe Doctrine— a proclamation declaring that if any other nation in this hemisphere asked to be annexed by the United States, such surrender of sovereignty was not open to European interference. Consequently, it might be concluded that when foreign critics speak of American imperialism, they are probably referring to the events surrounding the Spanish-American War. One might cite as representative in this connection

H. G. Wells' observation that the United States "came nearest to imperialism of the Great Power type" around the turn of the century in the Philippine Islands.

Here an examination is in order of the question of whether or not there exists a qualitative difference between the American and European varieties of imperialism. As far as the negative position is concerned, Salvador de Madariaga asserts that "American diplomats and American admirals, most of them anglo-maniacs, particularly when they disliked England by a psychological compensation, saw to it that the United States developed an entirely unnecessary Empire and a wholly unnecessary navy." This remark, pointing up our ambivalent attitude towards Britain, reflects the extent to which the American government relied on the English navy to enforce the Monroe Doctrine during the nineteenth century. In addition, it reveals that American imperialism, when it is accused abroad of being imitative, is usually regarded as a British variant rather than as a German or French or Italian product. Other of our critics concur in the judgment of de Madariaga that this country patterned its imperialist ventures on those of England.

In contrast, the belief that American imperialism does manifest certain original features has found support in many quarters. Thus Amaury de Riencourt writes that "no one could foresee at the turn of the century that European colonialism was an antiquated formula that would have to be replaced by a new type of imperialism—more responsible, more universal in scope, more subtle, and in the end more generous and more effective than any devised so far." De Riencourt also makes the rather enigmatic observation that American imperialism was actually the work of the anti-imperialist element. Along a more cynical line, Philip Guedalla declares that this new style American imperialism "advances under cover of a vigorous protestation of belief in the essential independence of the coveted object—and to lend it money." This view reflects the hypothesis that American imperialists often effect their ends through non-political means. It should be suggested that the characterizations of American imperialism offered by de Riencourt and Guedalla do not necessarily invalidate the ideas of de Madariaga noted in the last paragraph; both sets of observations are, in fact, valid provided that they are applied to the proper era of American history. The Spanish-American War might be suggested as a possible dividing line between the periods of political and ideological imperialism.

Some European commentators maintain that the United States

never has been imperialist except for a short period in its evolution. Such prominent foreign observers as Raymond Aron and Bertrand Russell adhere to this belief. The theory that imperialism is not the keynote of American foreign policy is aptly phased by Raymond Bruckberger, who notes that "a great hope for the world lies in the *elan* which I feel in this nation's response to the appeal of a universal vocation . . . it is entirely different from imperialistic ambition." In stressing the unselfish element inherent in our desire for world leadership, Bruckberger places his finger on a fact which European cynics have some difficulty in digesting, as they invariably interpret international relations in Machiavellian rather than Christian terms. Like Bruckberger, Andre Maurois holds that the U.S. "as a whole does not want colonial possessions or subject peoples"; he adds that the danger lies not in Americans exploiting a victim to whose aid they are rushing, but rather in their being swindled by a hypocrite who passes himself off as a victim. This consideration is often emphasized by American isolationists who oppose this nation becoming involved in international entanglements and it is often cited by our critics as one of the main dangers of an overly idealistic approach to foreign policy.

As the focal point of American imperialism has shifted from the political to the ideological sphere, the economic factor also has gained in importance. Thus the English historian Alfred Cobban remarks that "the basic facts of American imperialism are not political but economic, not the product of the will of the government, but of the commercial and financial activities of its citizens." Cobban adds that "while some small groups of individuals profited from it, other groups suffered economic injury." This observation creates a dilemma since it is almost impossible to determine the extent to which such gains and losses were the result of the operation of impersonal economic laws and to what degree they were by-products of imperialist maneuverings.

On the other hand, some European commentators recognize that the attempted correlation of American imperialism and American capitalism is not always supported by the facts. As Fritz Sternberg demonstrates, American monopoly capitalism was in the process of development prior to the period of the non-continental phase of American imperialism.[40] He also points out that imperialist undertakings have been of far less importance to the American economy than they have been to various European economies. It would be a mistake, however, to claim that American capitalism and American imperialism have never met in common cause, but this probably has happened less often than critics of the United States care to admit.

One factor that has hindered the development of imperialism in the United States is the political philosophy which permeates American life, as most critics regard democracy and imperialism as being theoretically incompatible. Thus Barbara Ward writes that "to assume a sustained and detailed strategy for any nation governed as is the United States is to assume the impossible." H. G. Wells similarly asserts that "there has hitherto existed in the States no organization for and no tradition of what one may call non-assimilable possessions." Ward and Wells also stress the openness with which foreign policy is debated in this country, an openness that makes difficult any imperialist ventures of the conspiratorial variety. Yet it must be admitted that in certain respects the foreign affairs of the United States are being conducted in a more secretive manner today than they were in the nineteenth century. Finally, as Bertrand Russell emphasizes, "annexation of territory has difficulties under the American Constitution"—a point well taken, for one could quite easily find numerous examples in American history to substantiate this position. These examples range from the indecision of Jefferson over whether the acquisition of the Louisiana Territory was constitutional to the question raised by the Insular Cases as to the status of Puerto Rico under the American Constitution.

There also exists a widespread belief abroad that a definite anti-colonial climate of opinion is currently operating in the United States. Here it might be observed that this country no longer has any colonies (or practically none), so that American anti-colonialists are in a spot where they are able to express anti-colonial sentiments without reflecting adversely on the United States. Andre Siegfried suggests that "to Americans Algeria is 'colonial', but neither Texas nor California is"—an observation that does much to explain this phenomenon. But it must be remembered that the overwhelming portion of the territory which the United States acquired when it was expanding was contiguous; thus to most Americans the word "colonialism" signifies possessions that are geographically far removed from the mother country. In addition, the United States was a colony of Great Britain prior to the time that it gained its independence; hence the American Revolution serves as a symbol of liberation to the freedom-seeking colonial areas. As Raymond Aron observes, "Americans sympathize with any revolt against foreign domination, even and particularly if this domination is exercised by a European ally."

It is not surprising that European commentators look with considerable bitterness upon the anti-colonial feeling which is in evidence here. This, moreover, has been a contributing factor to the hostility towards the United States currently widespread in Europe. Thus M. J. Bonn writes rather caustically that after World War II was over "and temporary Japanese domination had to be liquidated, American opinion with few exceptions almost invariably blamed the French, the Dutch, and the British on whom fell the task of turning chaos into order." It should be remembered that the American call for liberation from the Axis powers was widely interpreted throughout the colonial areas of the world as a pledge of their eventual independence; hence it is understandable that Europeans are rather touchy in regard to American criticisms of their colonial policies.

A slightly different approach is adopted by Max Beloff, who chides the United States for assuming that the colonial nations of Africa and Asia are capable of effecting a smooth transition from dependence to independence without falling into the hands of the communists. Such an assumption is a typical example of what Beloff and other European thinkers regard as an overly idealistic approach to foreign policy by the American government. Many foreign writers believe that the United States actually injures the cause of democracy by promoting colonial independence (Beloff is one of these), since an oligarchy will quite often seize control of those newly independent countries which lack the effective means of governing themselves. As a result, as Gunnar Myrdal observes, the United States is pushed "into alliance ... with reactionary personalities and social groups." This view, moreover, has been borne out numerous times in recent years, especially in what was once French Indo-China.

Having examined imperialism and its antithesis, anti-colonialism, we now turn to an analysis of isolationism. Despite the fact that they do not admire this phenomenon, most European observers acknowledge that the isolationist impulse is strongly rooted in the American soul. Thus Andre Siegfried declares that "the American by tradition is continentally minded," while Raoul de Roussy de Sales traces this impulse to "the tendency of America to consider itself not as an heir to or an extension of European civilization, but as an opposition to it." It is true that isolationism today is definitely on the wane in this country, but this does not imply that it is by any means a thing of the past. As Raymond Bruckberger observes, Americans "look back with nostalgia to the day when America had no world responsibilities." There exists a widespread awareness abroad that the United States has

abandoned isolationism with the greatest reluctance. Were it not for
the fact that, as G. D. H. Cole phrases it, "isolationism is no longer a
workable policy," there might be a clamor for a return to that ideology
under which this nation grew and developed in an atmosphere of relative peace.

A few words about the Monroe Doctrine is essential in any analysis
of American isolationism. In evaluating its historical significance,
Geoffrey Barraclough makes the observation that "the promulgation
of the Monroe Doctrine in 1823 meant definitely the exclusion of the
principle of the Balance of Power from the Americans." Amaury de
Riencourt similarly asserts that "the Monroe Doctrine implied a vir-
tual American protectorate over the entire Western hemisphere."
However, both de Riencourt's and Barraclough's remarks smack of
sour grapes, as one or more European nations would have moved in to
fill the vacuum had not the United States assumed the role of protector
of Latin America. That Latin America had as much, if not more, to
fear from Europe than it had from the United States is reflected in the
remark of Salvador de Madariaga that the Monroe Doctrine was
not wholly effective in thwarting European imperialism.

When a European observer refers to the isolationist component
of American foreign policy, he is probably thinking of the period
beween the rejection of the League of Nations and the disaster at
Pearl Harbor. It must be admitted that the abdication of international
responsibilities so characteristic of the nineteenth century United
States was the symptom of an isolationism as pronounced as that of its
more recent counterpart, but Europeans are mainly interested in
the twentieth century version of the isolationist impulse. This concern is explained partly by Barbara Ward's remark that the United
States at one time "had the geographical, economic, and political
means of being isolationist successfully," but that such is no longer
the case. Ward and many other European critics maintain that isolationism may have been the most logical policy for us to follow at one
time, but that it is no longer feasible and thus should be abandoned.
Of course, there is also an ulterior motive involved, as it is invariably
the European democracies that are especially concerned about American isolationism, since they have in recent years twice needed the
assistance of the United States to stave off the totalitarian menace.
This consideration effects to a marked degree the judgments of
European observers on American foreign policy.

It must be remembered that the term "isolationism" means different
things to different people. Thus such isolationists or former isolation-

ists as Robert Taft, Herbert Hoover, and Joseph Kennedy disagree on the extent to which isolationist policies should be implemented, and a distinction exists between isolationism *per se* and what Denis Brogan calls Pacific-centeredness. In addition, isolationism both here and abroad takes various forms, of which the diplomatic, economic, and cultural are the most important.

The present chapter is chiefly concerned with the diplomatic variety of American isolationism since it is this aspect which European commentators stress the most. Such an emphasis is not surprising; the Monroe Doctrine has been interpreted throughout American history primarily as a buffer against diplomatic intercourse, for it never was intended to be a damper on the exchange of goods or ideas. Moreover, the rejection of the League of Nations by the United States Senate demonstrates that twentieth century American isolationists are also concerned primarily with limiting diplomatic contacts.

One phenomenon which might be mentioned as an exception to this rule is the system of high tariffs which has been predominant at certain times in American history. Protectionism is related to isolationism to the degree that its supporters advocate economic self-sufficiency. Thus Henry Clay's simultaneous embracing of the Monroe Doctrine and the American System (which called for a high tariff) is a typical example of how the isolationist impulse may be correlated with protectionism. In recent years European observers have developed a particular aversion to American tariff walls. Writers of the stature of Harold Laski have even gone so far as to claim that American protectionism was a contributing factor to World War II, maintaining that by aggravating the world-wide economic crisis through a protective tariff this nation made possible the rise of dictatorships. But as Salvador de Madariaga points out, "the financial equilibrium of the world (was) frivolously disturbed by the men who drafted the reparations clauses of the Treaty." Thus the blame for the world's economic ills should not be placed entirely on the system of high tariffs in operation in the United States during the period from 1922 to 1933. Actually a rather low tariff rate has been in effect in this country since the latter date, so that observers abroad must admit that the American government did eventually modify its tariff policies so that they were more in line with European expectations. Moreover, European tariffs in the last generation or so have tended to move upward.

To the dyed-in-the-wool American isolationist, defeat of the League of Nations by the Senate was the truly great moment in American diplomatic history. This rejection was somewhat ironical in that the leader of the anti-League forces was not, strictly speaking, an isolationist. Moreover, Article 21 of the Covenant of the League was conceived by Woodrow Wilson as a world-wide extension of that cornerstone of isolationism, the Monroe Doctrine. Although European critics of American isolationism often charge that our rejection of the League was to prove disastrous when England and France made an attempt to halt the aggressions of Hitler, at least one observer (M. J. Bonn) takes issue with this claim. Bonn maintains that "the original opponents of the League convenant were people who distrusted pacifism, which they considered its guiding motive." In fact, quite a few people both here and abroad ignore the fact that many American isolationists were not opposed to blocking aggression, but felt that this country could obtain better results if it worked outside the framework of the League. As Salvador de Madariaga points out, the United States accepted the overwhelming majority of the principles for which the League stood,⁴ but preferred to conduct its international negotiations independently.

Taking into consideration the tremendous commotion that ensued in Europe after the United States Senate cast its vote against the League of Nations, it is quite surprising to find that many foreign observers feel either that this action was justified or that American participation in that organization would not have prevented war. H. G. Wells, for example, holds that "it was manifest that the people of America had no mind to a compact that was virtually little more than a league of allied imperialism for mutual insurance." Although Wells does admit that there may have been a sordid aspect to the American refusal to assume international responsibilities at this time, he writes that "the broad instinct of the American people seems to have been sound in its distrust of the proposed settlement." It is also noteworthy that those European commentators who criticize the American refusal to participate in the League of Nations often assume that the League was a near perfect cure-all for the world's problems. Such an assumption, of course, manifests an exaggerated idealism which European thinkers usually regard as characteristic of the United States rather than of themselves.

As for the theory that the League of Nations would have been more effective had America been an active member, Harold Laski claims that the real reason the League failed was because of its "subordinating of the obligations it imposed to the continued sovereignty of its members." Laski adds that "it is difficult to feel that the history of international relations between 1920 and 1939 would have been any different if the Senate had ratified the Treaty of Versailles without amendment." It must be remembered that the British and French governments were rather skeptical that they would be backed up by their peoples if they attempted any really drastic moves to halt the aggressions of Hitler. It is hardly likely, moreover, that the American citizenry, separated from Europe by thousands of miles of ocean, would have allowed their government to go even as far as the British and French populace did theirs. In addition, as J. A. Spender notes, "it was better for the United States to leave Europe to work out its own salvation in, at all events, the early stages of the League."⁴² This point is well taken. It is indeed conceivable that American interference in European affairs might have been received abroad with resentment rather than gratitude.

The strength of American isolationism in the years following Versailles is reflected in such a phenomenon as the rejection of the World Court scheme by Congress during the Harding, Coolidge, and Hoover Administrations. Even the Kellogg-Briand Pact outlawing war had a strong isolationist element, as is pointed out in the next chapter. The depression, moreover, probably had the effect of stimulating isolationism rather than discouraging it. Barbara Ward thus notes that "in the past, Americans have not sought to break economic deadlocks at home by conquering new markets abroad," and it is true that Congress enacted the highly protectionist Hawley-Smoot Tariff at that time (1930) instead of implementing free trade. F. D. R., of course, broke with the isolationists after a year or so in office, but early in his administration he dealt international economic cooperation a severe blow by refusing to take part in the London Economic Conference, as was mentioned in the eighth chapter.

Despite the fact that Franklin Roosevelt eventually attempted to direct this nation away from isolationism, the isolationist contingent remained numerous up until the attack on Pearl Harbor. Many Americans from all walks of life belonged to this group. Thus Harold Laski notes that its forces included "socialists like Norman Thomas, liberals like President Hutchins and Senator La Follette, reactionary priests like Father Coughlin and reactionary industrialists like Henry Ford and Generals Johnson and Wood." As might have been expected, the unwillingness of a large part of the citizenry of this nation to come to the aid of the European democracies quite naturally incited trans-Atlantic propagandists to a fever pitch, and it was in the days just prior to December 7, 1941 that European criticisms of the American isolationists reached their peak.

It is, of course, true that the Republican Mackinac Island Conference of 1943, U.S. participation in the United Nations in and after 1945, the Truman Doctrine of 1947, and the policies of the Eisenhower and Kennedy administrations have dealt major setbacks to American isolationism, but the isolationist element has by no means disappeared from the national scene.[43] During the so-called "Great Debate of the early 1950's attention centered around the question of American involvement in world affairs and it appears that isolationism now has become equated with an emphasis on the Pacific. This is not surprising when one considers that American expansion into this area during the nineteenth century was effected at a time when isolationism was at its peak here. In addition, the Republican Party has perhaps been more interested in the Pacific over the last century than has the Democratic and thus it was perhaps only natural that it would attack President Truman for putting too much stress on Europe.

European critics, of course, view with considerable distaste this new variety of American isolationism, and the reason for this is twofold. In the first place, the "Pacificists" would like to cut or reduce the ties between the United States and Europe. Secondly, foreign commentators generally feel that the school of thought represented by General MacArthur and ex-Senator Knowland is eager for this nation to become involved in a war with communist China. It is, of course, true that since the end of the Korean War the propaganda emanating from this group has steadily declined in intensity and frequency, but there still exists a fear overseas that American isolationism may rear its ugly head again in some other form. And judging from the past history of this phenomenon, one must conclude that this premonition is quite justified, although time alone will reveal the next shape that this ideological chameleon will take.

CHAPTER X

GLOBAL RESPONSIBILITIES

World War I is of crucial significance in the development of American foreign policy in that it was this event perhaps more than any other which was responsible for the assumption by the United States of a role of responsible world leadership. Admittedly the Venezuelan boundary and debt controversies and the Spanish-American War both resulted in the further involvement of this country in international politics, but World War I differed from these other events in that it brought into focus the question of permanent American entanglement in world affairs. It is true, of course, that in rejecting the League of Nations the Senate of the United States dealt internationalism a severe setback. However, the period during and just after World War I does mark the first concentrated attempt by this government to assist in charting the destiny of the remainder of the world through active intervention in global politics.

The underlying motives involved in the American participation in World War I by both Germany and England. As Guglielmo Ferrero a factor in the post-war attempt of the Wilson Administration to get the United States into the League of Naions. Despite the fact that they are overshadowed by the latter, an examination of these motives provides one with a clue as to how this apparent break with the past in American foreign policy was to a certain degree a continuation of prior trends. Actually, as J. A. Spender points out, "all through the last century and down to the entry of America into the Great War, the contentions of Great Britain and the United States have been largely about sea-power and its uses." Thus the controversy over the question of freedom of the seas which reached a climax in 1917 was one whose roots reached far into the past. In addition, the American "right" of freedom of the seas was threatened just prior to World War I by both Germany and England As Guglielmo Ferrero observes, "in 1915 and 1916 America found herself in conflict with England and Germany both at the same time and for the same reasons with the result that she should logically have declared war on both of them." But this did not happen. The question of why the United States went to war against Germany instead of England is one meriting further examination.

Both H. G. Wells and M. J. Bonn, as well as Raoul de Roussy de Sales, stress the importance of German submarine warfare as the instigating factor in American involvement in World War I. To be perfectly fair, however, it must be admitted that this freedom of the seas—submarine warfare hypothesis is not universally accepted as the sole consideration, as there are at least two other explanations which are also widely advocated by both European and American commentators. One of these theories emphasizes the so-called Teutonic menace. This is based on the assumption that the United States went to war to prevent a German victory which would have posed a danger to the whole world. In examining this possibility, Harold Laski states that "it had become clear by 1917 that a Germany which dominated Europe would be an expanding Germany, certain to dominate the Atlantic, and able in conjunction with Japan, to control the Pacific as well." Denis Brogan affirms in this connection that the real issue was not freedom of the seas, but rather that the British navy might be destroyed by the Germans, and it must be admitted that this country was long dependent on the English fleet.

The second of these theories, on the other hand, centers around the strong economic ties which existed in 1917 between the United States and several of the democracies of Europe (particularly England). As Raymond Aron comments, "economic participation became military partnership when the submarines tried to break the bond already existing between the European and American democracies," and Oswald Spengler also recognizes the role of the business interests in this conflict. This hypothesis has been twisted by the anti-Semites so as to infer that the great Jewish banking houses of Europe (the Rothchilds, etc.) dragged the United States into World War I, but such an interpretation deserves little credence despite the vigor with which it is supported in certain quarters.

There exists a nearly universal belief on this side of the Atlantic that the United States saved Europe from the German threat, but this opinion is not as widespread in Europe. Thus Raymond Aron admits that "General Pershing's divisions provided the reinforcements necessary to 'finish the job.' Nevertheless, to the very end, the French Army constituted the largest component of the Allied troops." Fritz Sternberg similarly writes that America's entry into World War I turned stalemate into victory, rather than defeat into triumph. John Maynard Keynes, on the other hand, maintains that the Ameri-

can financial contribution to the Allied cause during the war was of
more importance than its military aid; this remark might be related
to the hypothesis that financial ties between Europe and the United
States were a factor in America's involvement in World War I. It
is because of this assistance, both military and economic, that
Americans often boast that the United States rescued the European
democracies from the Teutonic menace, and this claim is widely resented abroad. The resulting misunderstanding, of course, did much
to hinder an agreement between this country and Europe on the
war debt question and other problems arising from World War I.

In regard to the internal impact of World War I on the United
States, one would have to agree with H. A. L. Fisher that this nation
was affected by the war to only a limited degree, as well as with Denis
Brogan that this conflict made less of an impression on the American
mind than the Civil War. But this does not mean that its impact was
strictly nil; few if any European commentators would go so far
as to make this assertion. Thus both Harold Laski and Philip Gibbs
claim that the war had an adverse effect on American life, as they
and quite a few other critics believe that the right of freedom of
speech was violated at this time. On the other hand, as the English
political scientist Graham Wallas points out, compulsory military
service here was not widely considered abroad as a violation of personal liberty, probably because of its long tradition in many European
countries.

From the economic point of view, Andre Tardieu and many other
European writers have often stressed that World War I stimulated
the American economy; this conflict admittedly helped to solidify the
position of the United States as a creditor nation. It is bitterly resented abroad that Americans generally speak of the great sacrifices which
they made in participating in this war, while they also boast
of the size of the profits they accumulated. As to the effect of
the war on the national character, Hermann von Keyserling
echoes a widespread sentiment in his claim that "*America as a whole
has for the first time become conscious of her individual soul.*" It is
indeed ironic that a period of closer diplomatic ties between the Old
World and the New would be accompanied by a corresponding
spiritual alienation, but such was the case, as it is generally recognized
that the United States finally "broke away" from Europe at this time.

Despite the fact that he did as much, if not more, than Franklin
Roosevelt to project the United States into a position of responsible
world leadership, Woodrow Wilson has fared far less well at the hands

of European critics than has F. D. R. When thinking of Wilson
one is reminded of the observation Voltaire once made in regard to
Charles XII of Sweden that the latter carried his virtues to the
point where they became less desirable than their corresponding vices.
The classic portrayal of Wilson as a great idealist but an inept politician is probably the one found in John Maynard Keynes' *The Economic Consequences of the Peace,* but even the Wilsonian idealism has
been questioned by more than one European thinker of note. Amaury
de Riencourt, for example, writes that "Wilson behaved like a party
politician and yet talked to the world like an inspired prophet"; this
remark is in obvious reference to Wilson's message to the people
calling for the election of a Democratic Congress in 1918. It must
be noted that many of the European criticisms of Wilson display
poor judgment or faulty reasoning. One must, for example, question
the correctness of the 1919 observation of M. J. Bonn that Wilson's
eventual place in history was dependent on his success. Harold
Laski confuses influence with individuality in his observation that the
effect of Wilson on foreign policy formulation has been overrated,
since he was not an original thinker.[44] Other negative judgments may
not be brushed aside so easily; some of these will now be analyzed.

An examination of the numerous points contained in the Wilsonian
program of world reorganization reveals that quite a few of these
items, despite their nobility of purpose, have been regarded abroad
as ultimately having an adverse effect. Thus Raoul de Roussy de
Sales writes that "in proclaiming the right of national self-determination, Wilson did not prepare the way for the liberation of the people
from tyranny; he gave a stimulus to nationalism and, quite un-
wittingly, paved the road for the extreme revolutionary claims of
Hitler and Mussolini." Alfred Cobban similarly poses the question
of whether or not it was ethical for the principle of self-determination
to be applied to the vanquished and not also to the victors. Also
of significance in this connection is the observation of de Roussy
de Sales that Wilson rather than the Kaiser was the true revolutionary in World War I. Americans often claim that the United States
entered the war on the side of the Allies because a German victory
would have resulted in a wholesale rearrangement of world politics,
but the Allied powers under the leadership of Wilson were the ones
who supported sweeping changes after the war.

The analysis of the defeat of the League of Nations by the United
States Senate which was presented in the last chapter pointed out that
this action was a result of the resurgence of isolationism here. Despite

this rejection, it is indeed debatable whether this nation was in a position at this time to exert really effective world leadership. Thus M. J. Bonn points out that once America had won the war, it had lost most of the bargaining power which it once used as a means of dealing with the democracies of Europe. Accordingly, the United States was not able to obtain a great many of its objectives at the peace conference held at Versailles. As Guglielmo Ferrero notes, the fact that Wilson could not get France and England to agree to implement the American position on the question of freedom of the seas meant that to this extent the American participation in World War I was useless. Many observers, in fact, maintain that had this country decided to play an active role in world affairs after 1918 that it would have had to have been as a partner of England and France rather than as their leader. It is, of course, debatable whether the American people would have consented to such a subordination of their interests to those of Europe even if the League of Nations had been approved by the Senate.

Of all the attempts which the American government made between the two world wars to aid the cause of peace, it is perhaps the Kellogg-Briand Pact which was the most praised, yet at the same time there probably was no other effort which was so widely criticized in Europe. This may, indeed, seem paradoxical, but it must be remembered that European observers saw no plausible reason for the United States to sign the Kellogg-Briand Pact and yet not enforce it through League of Nations. Thus Salvador de Madariaga cynically remarks that this nation "prefers to keep her idealism uncontaminated and, like the old lady in *Punch*, thinks the League is very nice but too full of foreigners." H. G. Wells similarly states that the Kellogg-Briand Pact "is just another place of empty, fruitless American 'idealism' utterly worthless to the world at large," while Norman Angell asks why the signing of this agreement was followed almost immediately by "legislation authorizing a very great increase in American naval power." It is highly probable that the Kellogg-Briand Pact was the result of a "sense of duty somehow neglected or evaded," as Alfred Zimmern suggests. It should be remembered that American isolationists often compensate for their advocacy of diplomatic estrangement from Europe by crusading in behalf of moral and ethical principles. This is as true of American isolationists today as it was of their nineteenth century counterparts.

One of the most controversial aspects of American foreign policy between the two world wars concerns the relative degree of friendliness between England and the United States during this period. On the one hand, Andre Siegfried writes that Great Britain was the one European nation which was able to lay claim to a favored position in American diplomatic dealings,[45] while on the other, H. G. Wells declares that there existed a strong possibility of war between these two countries during this period. Although the position taken by Siegfried and others is probably the generally accepted one, it is noteworthy that many European writers think as Wells does on this issue. Thus Hilaire Belloc reflects British hostility in his remark that an Anglo-American alliance would have seriously weakened England, while Guglielmo Ferrero asserts that the United States faced a challenge from England (and Japan) rather than from Germany. An additional factor inimical to friendly Anglo-American relations was that a widespread opinion existed in Great Britain at this time that Americans were rather critical of the way that the British handled their Empire. This is especially true of India, as Philip Gibbs and various other European writers frequently emphasize. It may seem rather strange today that relations between this nation and England during these two decades should have been hostile, but they were so at times. This explains in part why the United States did not come rushing to the aid of England in the middle 1930's when Germany was again developing into a threat to world peace.

The fact that Franklin Roosevelt was an isolationist early in his Presidency makes it appear inconsistent that he is almost invariably regarded abroad as the leading advocate of the Allied cause in pre-World War II days, although such is the case. Raymond Aron, for example, writes of the isolationist opposition in America to the "enlightened" international policies of F. D. R., observing that "Roosevelt was reduced to the prediction of a catastrophe which he might have been able to prevent."[46] Considering the Rooseveltian vacillations in the field of world affairs, it is indeed puzzling that it is F. D. R. and not Wilson whom many Europeans hold in the highest esteem. A possible answer to this apparent inconsistency lies in the fact that Europeans do not feel that the American intervention prevented the defeat of the European democracies during World War I, but that it did avert such a catastrophe in the second global conflict. Franklin Roosevelt has achieved this rating despite the fact that the United States did not become a participant in this conflict until two years after its European phase had begun, and although it might not even have become involved had it not been attacked.

As might be expected, there are those foreign critics who assign some of the blame for World War II to the United States. Thus Harold Laski writes of "the desertion of Europe after Versailles, the hindrances to the free migration of peoples, (and) the disastrous economic nationalism in which the United States has been a pioneer." The majority of European thinkers are kind enough to admit that the democracies of Europe have not been free from sin, either. Laski points out elsewhere that America did not engage in World War II for purely ideological reasons, but rather because this country was forced to fight in self-defense, and it might be added that this was true of World War II even more than it was of World War I. Moreover, the fact that the United States for the second time assumed the role of savior of the world with reluctance is vividly reflected in the deluge of books and articles which European commentators produced in 1939 and after imploring this nation to give military or economic assistance to their countries. The propaganda of Norman Angell, Fritz Sternberg, and Harold Laski is rarely profound, but it bears witness to American unwillingness to become involved internationally as late as 1941.

One must agree with Fritz Sternberg that although America was the least prepared for war of all the belligerents in 1939, it still possessed the greatest potential of all the nations which took part in World War II. In fact, quite a few persons both here and abroad maintain that another depression might have occurred in the United States had it not been for the outbreak of this global conflict.[47] Arnold Toynbee similarly observes that World War II greatly accelerated the industrialization of the South, and it is probably true that the war did more for the economic development of Dixie (and the rest of America as well) than such New Deal measures as the Tennessee Valley Authority. This mushrooming economic growth perhaps impresses European analysts more than any other result of the impact of World War II on this country, although, as was the case after World War I, there was widespread bitterness abroad that America thus prospered while Europe suffered economically.

When World War II ended in 1945 with a German defeat and the establishment of the United Nations, the hopes of the internationalists reached an all-time high, but their dreams were soon crushed by the emergence of the communist threat. It was pointed out in the seventh chapter that many European commentators did not immediately recognize the danger that the Soviet Union posed to the peace of the world, and they are thus rather sensitive to the charge that they are not vigilant enough in fighting the communist menace. Moreover, such foreign thinkers as Harold Laski often compensate for the inadequate efforts of Europe in combating communism by accusing this country of leading the world into a third global conflict through its "aggressive" policies. The Korean War did modify sentiment in that it made it apparent to the free nations that America rather than Russia was their friend, but one still is able to detect undercurrents of resentment against the United States even to the present day. This hostility is reflected in the recent prestige polls which reveal a lowered estimate of America abroad.

Of all American post-World War II policies, it is perhaps the foreign aid program (in particular the Marshall Plan) and the atomic monopoly which initially caused the most controversy in European circles, while the satellite race, which is discussed in the postscript, has attained an increasing prominence in recent years. In regard to the Marshall Plan, Barbara Ward makes the significant comment that "the two factors—Marshall (Plan) aid and Western association— are essentially distinct." It is true that American assistance to the democracies of Western Europe does not guarantee that these European nations will work together, but these two concepts are so closely allied in the mind of the average American that he is likely to become upset when he perceives that there is no mandatory correlation between them. M. J. Bonn similarly observes that the Marshall Plan in its original form was not strictly intended as a move to halt the expansion of communism. Bonn adds that it was primarily an attempt to aid the war damaged economies of Europe, and it probably would have been formulated whether there had been a communist threat or not. This consideration has often been overlooked in the United States.

In discussing the reception which Europeans accorded to the Marshall Plan, Denis Brogan notes that there is a widespread feeling in Europe that the assistance provided under the Plan "was a mere drop in the bucket of what we were owed by the Americans, inadequate and pharisaical conscience money." On the other hand, there also exists an awareness abroad that the nations of Europe have been strengthened by this assistance, and this sentiment is perhaps as widespread as the other. As Arnold Toynbee observes, if the Marshall Plan is a success, the result will be the construction of an economic system embracing the whole world (with the exception of the Soviet sphere) under the leadership of the United States. Although Toynbee may have made an excessive claim in his prediction, many other thinkers abroad concur in Toynbee's judgment that it has had a beneficial

economic effect on Europe. Barbara Ward, however, disagrees with
Toynbee in that she believes that "in spite of this remarkable material
achievement, the greatest significance of the Marshall Plan lies in
the sphere of social containment." It would seem, therefore, that it
has been received with as varied a reaction abroad as here, although
attention is being shifted today to other phases of our foreign aid
program.

In view of the circulation of the Stockholm Peace Petition throughout Europe, one might expect that the major objection that Europeans would have to American military policy would be its reliance
on atomic weapons. Raymond Bruckberger, for example, writes
that "the rest of the world remains unconvinced that you were compelled to drop the bomb." But it appears that Europeans are as much
disturbed by America's failure to share our atomic secrets with its
European allies as by its stockpiling of nuclear devices. As Raymond
Aron observes, the American decision to withold certain atomic
information from its allies has done little to bolster (if indeed it has
not injured) the confidence of the members of the free world in
each other.

Other criticisms of this country's atomic policy should also be noted.
Harold Laski, for example, maintains that under "the American plan"
for the international control of atomic energy Russia would be a
minority member of the International Atomic Authority without the
power of veto, so that the United States would be in a position to
control this body.[48] Unfortunately, Laski does not specify what particular plan he is referring to (there were several), so that his remark
is rather vague. In addition, there exists a widespread sentiment in
Europe that America desires to preserve the *status quo* in the atomic
race because this country has the most to gain from this arrangement.
It must be admitted, nevertheless, that the atomic bomb is not available as an offensive weapon to the American government, as Raymond
Aron points out, since public opinion in this nation would not very
likely consent to its use except in self-protection. Commenting
further, Aron observes that "it is difficult to resist the impression that
the United States has lost rather than gained by its famous atomic
monopoly," and many Americans concur in this opinion.

Considering the importance of the adverse judgments which European observers have levelled against our foreign aid program and our
atomic policy, an examination of certain other criticisms of American
foreign policy is in order. One of the more noteworthy of these is that
this country injures the cause of freedom by supporting the leading

reactionaries of Europe. Representative in this connection is Fritz Sternberg's observation that this association creates "a social situation that will help the communists and Russians to shattering successes." Sternberg's remark is obviously directed against the dealings which the American government has had with the dictatorship now in control of Spain, although there are quite a few other examples which might be mentioned Another widespread criticism which European commentators often make is that the United States hopes to solve all the problems of the world overnight. As Luigi Barzini remarks, "there is nothing wrong with all these American initiatives," but "what is wrong *is* the Americans' hopes of immediate success." It should be recalled, moreover, that many analysts of the American character regard impatience as a typically American trait, and Americans are obviously as impatient with foreigners as with each other.

In addition, one might cite various other negative evaluations of American foreign policy. Harold Laski, for example, asserts that the United States hampers the effectiveness of the United Nations by developing such programs as aid to Greece and Turkey without consulting that organization. This criticism is perhaps unfair, since there do occur times when this country may more effectively promote the cause of world peace by by-passing the United Nations. Moreover, when one considers that European commentators often assail the idealistic features of American foreign policy, it is ironical that they also attack the realistic approach which George Kennan advocates, but such is the case. R. H. S. Crossman thus writes that Bismarckian realism may be just as disastrous a policy for the peace of the world as Wilsonian utopianism, so that the United States is seemingly criticized regardless of whether it bases its foreign policy on either idealistic or realistic principles.

Indeed, one wonders whether this government will ever be able to work out a global program which will be entirely satisfactory to the democracies of Europe. On the one hand, Europeans fear that too aggressive an American foreign policy might detonate a war with Russia, while on the other, too weak a one might encourage further Soviet aggressions. As a result, they try to steer a middle of the road course which is widely interpreted in the United States as a sign of muddleheadedness, despite the fact that it is actually a carefully designed balancing act calculated to play both ends against the middle. Since this nation has been rather uncompromising as to foreign policy in the age of isolationism as well as in that of internationalism, it is difficult for Americans to sympathize with what most of them regard as an expedient approach.

Moreover, there is a realization in Europe that the future of the world does not rest in its hands as it once did. Despite the fact that Denis de Rougemont writes of global leadership that the United States "has not sought such a responsibility, and it is not equipped to shoulder it," most European thinkers are aware that America, and not Europe, will lead the forces of freedom in the future. As Luigi Barzini observes, "whether she likes it or not, whether she acknowledges it or refuses to face the fact, all her decisions, even the small, insignificant and private ones, have world-wide repercussions." Denis Brogan likewise admits that the United States may not succeed, but remarks that there are two orders of risk, "the risk of certain disaster if nothing is done, and the risk of failure if something is attempted." Brogan obviously prefers the second alternative.

But judging by the numerous forces at work in the world today, it is fallacious to assume that the United States will dictate the destiny of mankind in the years to come. As Fritz Sternberg notes, "it cannot be the aim of American foreign policy to oppose the great process of transformation that is going on throughout Asia and Europe today." In fact, it sometimes seems that the government of this country is perplexed as to how to deal with the evolving problems of humanity, such as the decline of colonialism and the rise of newly independent nations. It is, moreover, quite likely that American foreign policy may take some rather strange turns in the future;[49] the fact that isolationism and imperialism have been superseded by internationalism is no guarantee that complexity or paradox is a thing of the past in American foreign relations. For that matter, it is not probable that European attitudes towards the foreign policies of this nation will undergo any wholesale simplification in the future as new dilemmas are continually making their appearance on the international horizon.

CHAPTER XI

RELIGION ON TRIAL

The intensity of American religiosity is one of the most hotly debated aspects of life on this side of the Atlantic. European observers are in considerable disagreement as to whether or not the United States is a truly religious nation, since the question of whether the outward manifestation and the inner spirit are necessarily correlated here is a matter of controversy. The fact that the term "spirituality" is sometimes used interchangeably with "religiosity" and in other instances as an independent concept only complicates matters, since the expressions "religious" and "spiritual" are not synonymous. Thus Salvador de Madariaga ignores the religious element in his observation that America is characterized by a "spiritual oneness," while "spiritually, Europe is not one." The term "religious", however, will be employed almost exclusively throughout this chapter, and it is hoped that this usage will help to clarify matters.

A typical expression of the sentiment that Americans are essentially religious is Jacques Maritain's assertion that "a deep-rooted, sometimes hidden, sometimes unconscious, but actual and alive religious inspiration is embodied in the temporal, secular, lay life of this country." This remark is striking in that the religion of which Maritain is such a distinguished spokesman (Catholicism) is a minority faith in America. Thus his opinion obviously is not based on a narrow, denominational bias. As for the expression of the religious spirit in tangible form here, one might cite the remark of J. A. Spender that "whether for Christian missions abroad, distressed and starving foreign nations, Community funds, Church buildings, or Mississippi floods at home, there is no appeal which seems to fail of an instant and generous response." This is a typical appraisal of the extent that the Christian faith is implemented by works in America, and thus serves as a complement to those observations dealing with the fruits of contemplation.

The above observations are of importance, but one must examine the logic sustaining such statements before passing a definitive judgment on American religiosity. In this connection, Raymond Bruckberger presents a rather negative argument in his claim that the absence of atheism from the United States is the result of a deficient historical tradition, while Richard Muller-Freienfels asserts that the power of religion here is attributable to the fact that Americans are less critically perceptive than are Europeans. But a more positive theory might be suggested. Thus one could reasonably claim that introspection and abstract thought are likely to breed religious skepticism, and this has taken place more in Europe than it has in America. On the other hand, extroversion and pragmatic thinking will probably produce an outwardly religious outlook, and this has occurred to a greater extent in the United States than it has in Europe.

Moreover, those European writers who are convinced of the essential religiosity of America often offer such explanations as to give one the impression that the foundations on which American piety rest are either negative or non-spiritual. Thus in the course of an imaginary dialogue between Voltaire and a man from Sirius, Salvador de Madariaga has the French philosopher exclaim that the Americans are the "most richly endowed in faith" of any people in the world. Yet the fictional Voltaire also makes the rather sarcastic observation (in obvious reference to Mary Baker Eddy and Christian Science) that "one of their race, a woman, decided that a new system of medicine was to spring from the Bible; and behold! the system was there, up and doing, undistinguishable from other medical systems in its mortiferous effects." Hermann von Keyserling, who similarly finds Americans to be religious, observes that "if earth-bound America is primitive, so must spiritual America be" and adds that "American life is bent on the conquest and rule of matter as no life ever has been before." To von Keyserling it is only natural that such a religion as Christian Science should have developed in the United States. If true, these remarks establish credulity and primitivism as among the cornerstones of religion in this country, and they and similar comments give one the impression that America has taken the right position on religion, but for the wrong reasons.

Even those European critics who admit that religiosity in this nation is at a high level frequently write of the large number of Americans who do not hold church memberships. Thus Lucien Romier and Andre Lafond estimate the number of church non-members in the United States at fifty million individuals. Viewed in a broader perspective, it is quite ironical that European thinkers castigate Americans for their quantitative rather than qualitative standards of judgment, yet often determine the extent of American religiosity (either pro or con) on the basis of statistics. On the other hand, in observing that "for the American, religion is generally either an empty form of worship . . . or the exercise of a prejudice" Lucien Lehman comes to his conclusions without the benefit of a slide rule or a calculating machine. There are many other European critics who challenge the claim that this is a religious nation; some of their opinions in this connection will now be examined.

In reflecting on the panorama of American life, Denis de Rougement complains of "plains and cities equally immense, devoid of mystery, cleansed of all trace of primitive religion and of any veneration for things, plants, animals or the supernatural." To de Rougemont both Russia and the United States are spiritually regressive, while Europe alone offers "the recipe for balance" to the individual.

Criticisms of the religious state of affairs in this country are by no means confined to European Protestants such as de Rougemont; they also permeate the writings of such confirmed agnostics as Bertrand Russell. Thus Russell observes that "the old pious formulas are repeated on Sundays, and are thought, by those who repeat them, to be still believed," but "they have become only Sunday truths, and during the rest of the week other views prevail." Both de Rougemont's and Russell's remarks accentuate the difference between appearance and reality, and in both instances the United States is downgraded religiously as the result of this distinction.

The attitudes of those European observers who maintain that religion is losing its hold on American life often reflect a preoccupation with the concepts of "secularization" and "socialization." As to secularization, Denis Brogan remarks that theology with its stress on God has given way to anthropology with its emphasis on man, while Harold Laski concludes that many recent religious thinkers have molded the tenets of the church to fit the problems facing the world.[50] In reference to socialization, Rom Landau comments that "churchianity" is essentially a social convention with most people, while Odette Keun observes that churches are today preponderantly social institutions rather than religious organizations. The implication of these theories is, of course, that the highest forms of religion are other-worldly and individual-centered, or that they place greater emphasis on these focal points than on the secular and social ones. This view has as yet to be proven correct, but it is nevertheless widespread abroad, and is often used in arguments which question American religiosity.

Since many of them regard the religious impulse of this nation to be rather superficial, it is not surprising that European analysts frequently maintain that Americans do not have a very profound under!standing of good and evil. As Simone de Beauvoir observes, "they could not even imagine a situation in which they could have been forced to contribute to an evil," since "people here refuse to do this, even though it is the only way to fight evil."[51] Or as Jacques Maritain sums up the situation, "in other words, there is no hidden root of evil in our nature, no original sin, no need for divine grace." Maritain's assertion is, of course, in obvious reference to the influence of Rousseau on American thought. It might be asserted in rebuttal to these observations that the fact that the sense of evil is possibly more developed in Europe than it is in the United States may only prove that Europe has been exposed more to war and pestilence than has this country. The absence of those conditions from America which give rise to a deeper understanding of evil may, in fact, demonstrate that the inner goodness of man is greater here than elsewhere, rather than that this nation is spiritually deficient.

Skepticism is also widely regarded abroad as being outside the experience of the average American. In analyzing various comments on its absence from the United States, one encounters such expected remarks as that Americans are credulous or that they do not approach life intellectually enough. Raoul de Roussy de Sales, on the other hand, maintains that "today one seldom meets an American skeptic for the reason that nothing is more assuredly un-American than to entertain any doubt concerning the fact that somehow or other this country will come out all right."[52] In the section on democracy it was pointed out that many European writers believe that the American way of life has taken on certain of the characteristics of religion, and thus a correlation of faith in the political and religious spheres is quite logical. For this reason, it is only to be expected that the skeptical attitude towards existence is the exception rather than the rule in the United States, and that, as Hilaire Belloc asserts, it has not done much damage to the fundamentally Puritan ethical tradition of this country.

But Europeans do not always correlate the relative absence of skepticism from this nation with a corresponding lack of anti-clericalism. This is only logical in that the latter is occasionally in evidence here. In writing of the anti-clerical tradition in America, Denis Brogan refers to the widespread criticisms directed against the Methodist Board of Temperance, Prohibition, Public Morals, and the Catholic hierarchy in general. These two groups appear to be the leading scapegoats in this controversy.

It is significant, too, that it is European free thinkers rather than

European religious leaders who emphasize this anti-clerical agitation here most strongly. This is for the reason that many European liberals correlate anti-clericalism with democracy, and thus are vitally interested in the setbacks that organized religion suffers in the United States. They, of course, have American counterparts.

Before analyzing the more modern forms of American Protestantism, it is necessary to examine the historical significance of Puritanism. It must be remembered that the Puritan and the pioneer are widely regarded as the two most important representative types in the historical development of the United States. As for the early years of this nation, Hermann von Keyserling observes of Puritanism that "this spiritual force alone was strong enough to counteract the influence of the American soil and thus to make for the preservation of the ancestral type." Puritanism, however, was no unmixed blessing. As Arnold Toynbee points out, the Puritans reacted to the role that they played as persecutees in England by turning into persecutors themselves when they became established in the New World. Yet despite its shortcomings, Puritanism is still a major force in the United States, at times somewhat disguised in form, but often influencing society to a marked extent.

Most European commentaters recognize that the sense of original sin so predominant in Puritanism has greatly affected various forms of regulatory legislation (such as Prohibition) which have been enacted in America. As Odette Keun writes, "it is difficult otherwise to account for the exceptional multiplicity of ordinances, the half-heartedness with which they are put through, and the passivity with which public opinion accepts their ultimate futility." Although the overwhelming majority of writers abroad correlate original sin with pessimism, Hermann von Keyserling expresses the view that Puritan moralism has led to modern optimism. Von Keyserling doubtless could find many supporters for his theory among those psychologists who emphasize the idea of compensation, but his opinion is decidely a minority one. It might also be suggested that the sense of original sin is more widespread in the United States than one would suspect, since it probably is a factor in such seemingly unrelated phenomena as our guilt feelings stemming from this nation taking an inadequate role in world affairs.

The Puritan doctrine of predestination has likewise been an important theme in American history. As Oswald Spengler observes in one of his more lucid moments, "it formed that which may be called the American religion of today, and bred and fostered the trait which gives the Englishman even now his particular political insouciance, an assurance that is essentially religious and has its roots in predestination." It is to this, rather than to the doctrine of original sin, that the optimistic outlook of modern American society should probably be traced. Significantly, there are few European commentators who label the American state of mind as fatalistic, since fatalism is a form of predestination which usually involves passive resignation before future events. It, therefore, does not carry with it the assurance of success which is so characteristic of the American variety of Calvinism.

Aside from the manifestations of predestination and original sin, numerous other features of American life have been traced to Puritanism. In summarizing some of these, Harold Laski refers to "the regard for effort, the belief that success attends upon it, the suspicion that failure is due to some defect of character, the justification of wealth as a stewardship . . . the dislike of radical doctrines as a social form of anti-nomianism, (and) the fear of any ideas which may bring into jeopardy the unity of the commonwealth." Similarly, in asserting that Americanism is an amalgam of Puritanism, Enlightenment philosophy, and mechanization, Amaury de Riencourt writes that "moralism, with its implied good faith and reliability, is the foundation of all prosperous business life, and business is America's primary occupation." Laski's and de Riencourt's observations explaining how secular endeavor in this nation is often justified on religious grounds are not the only ones that might be listed, moreover, as Max Weber and R. H. Tawney have developed this point more extensively on a supra-national basis.

But, despite the important role that Puritanism has played in American life, many European thinkers regard it to be on the decline today as an effective social force. Andre Maurois attributes this decrease in potency to such factors as "middle-class respectability, sentimentalism and prudery," as well as to the development of modern science and "modernist" religion. Hermann von Keyserling similarly opines that Puritanism has little chance of survival, "since its tenets are in complete contradiction with the general modern outlook." But Von Keyserling does believe that it will remain an element in the American collective unconscious. Denis Brogan's recent assessment of Los Angeles as no longer being puritanical also supports the hypothesis that Puritanism is on the decline, since it reverses a judgment made by him twenty years earlier that this was the most puritancial of large American cities. One might cite many other observations supporting this point as well.

Yet whatever may be their appraisals of the desirability of the Puritan world view, foreign commentators invariably speak of Puritanism with respect. This is not always the case with the Fundamentalist variety of American Protestantism, as such widely ridiculed phenomena as Prohibition and anti-evolution laws have been generally identified with it. Moreover, European critics are frequently quite sarcastic in their observations on the more primitive forms of American Protestantism. One, in fact, encounters such anecdotes as that about the individual who left the Catholic church for free thought, and who, when asked why he did not become a Protestant, replied that he had lost only his faith, not his reason. This scorn also permeates the more "objective" observations of European analysts. Thus Bernard Fay writes of Fundamentalist austerities that "all sorts of groups—young women, old maids, young men, married men, etc.—made it their mission to impose on themselves or their neighbors some privation or another supposed to be moral." Such a remark, however, is not a condemnation of self-denial but is rather a criticism of a series of acts where Fay believes that the self-denial effected no higher ends, regardless of the good intentions which underlay it.

Predictably those Protestant religious organizations and spokesmen which are the most alien to the modern spirit bear the brunt of this attack. In evaluating certain aspects of the contemporary American religious scene. Hermann Von Keyserling acidly commented that "Christian Science, from the scientific point of view, is a form of Shamanist religion; Fundamentalism is one of the crudest expressions of Tabooism I know of; and the Reverend Billy Sunday plays upon the instruments of the savage tribesman's fear-mechanism with the most consummate skill." Von Keyserling's observation, moreover, is a representative expression of the widespread point of view that the emotional element in religion should be subordinated to the intellectual component.

This pronounced European distaste for certain manifestations of the religious spirit here is usually accompanied by a sigh of relief, as it appears inconceivable to Europeans that the present conditions will endure much longer. Thus Andre Siegfried asserts that "on the whole, modernism has conquered, although it is not considered good to describe oneself as liberal." One must admit, of course, that the current trend appears to be away from Fundamentalism in America, but it is equally indisputable that the Bible Belt is still in business. It would seem, therefore, that its liquidation in the near future is quite unlikely, despite the trans-Atlantic verbal barrage that has been directed against it.

The membership of the Catholic Church in the United States is numerically greatly inferior to that of the combined forces of Protestantism. Nevertheless, Catholicism has influenced the course of American life to a degree disproportionate to its relative strength. In comparing the Old World and the New, Hilaire Belloc observes that the dividing line between Protestant and Catholic culture in America is practically indiscernible, while such a line does exist in Europe. Moreover, the relationship between the Catholic Church and the various national states is not the same in the Old World as it is in the New. Thus Belloc refers to the fact that in Europe there has been a struggle between the Ultramontanists, who advocate Papal supremacy, and the Erastians, who support the ultimate authority of the state. In America, on the other hand, there has been no protracted battle between the dominant religion (Protestantism) and the government, mainly because church and state are separated under the Constitution. There are, of course, various similarities between the religious state of affairs in the United States and Europe, but foreign commentators seemingly emphasize the points of contrast more strongly.

A striking demonstration of the extent to which European critics differ in their comments on the roles of Protestantism and Catholicism in the New World is reflected in their observations on the so-called "moral" question. As far as the use of intoxicating beverages here is concerned, Bernard Fay claims that "Catholicism has not allowed itself to be dragged into politics like the Protestant churches, which, in order to retain prohibition, have been compelled to mingle in political struggles to their own great detriment." On the other hand, Denis Brogan refers to the "Catholic zeal over the suppression of indecent books, opposition to easy divorce, (and) the importation of Irish sexual prudery." Assuming that both assertions are correct one might conclude that the moral zeal of one faith is concentrated against alcohol and that of the other against immorality. But this leaves open the question of the intensity of the fanatical spirit of each organization; no one as yet seems to have measured this for comparative purposes, although most European anti-clericals doubtless feel that both religious bodies are far too zealous.

Another extremely controversial issue is the degree to which the

Catholic Church has advanced the cause of conservatism in this
country. Many European leftist thinkers support the thesis that
Catholicism has been the ally of the political right here. Thus Harold
Laski charges that "the Roman Catholic Church is, if indirectly, one
of the strongest influences in the United States against any large-scale
effort at change." Various European spokesmen for this religious body
naturally tend to resent this claim, although Catholics frequently are as
extreme in their remarks as is Laski in his. A simple resolution of
this problem is highly difficult, however, as one is able to detect both
conservative and liberal elements at work in American Catholicism.
Thus Msgr. John A. Ryan formulated ideas which were later incorpor-
ated into the New Deal, while the quasi-fascistic Father Coughlin ex-
postulated on the radio against the Rooseveltian reforms. There are,
moreover, conservative and liberal as well as reactionary and radical
currents present within American Protestantism, so that this political
divergence among Catholics is not unusual.

There also is considerable disagreement among European thinkers
in regard to the educational achievements of Protestantism and
Catholicism in the United States. Thus Bernard Fay quotes an "eminent Protestant" (unidentified by Fay) to the effect that the Catholic
church appears to be doing the best job of educating children
religiously here. On the other hand, Denis Brogan complains that
Catholics have contributed little to the intellectual development of
America. Of course, few critics would deny that Catholics are
better indoctrinated religiously in the United States than are Protestants. This, however, does not prove that they are also the leaders
in the field of general education here, as there are as many, if not more,
Harvards as Notre Dames. And, if one admits that the Catholic
Church has not produced many outstanding thinkers in the United
States, one must also recognize if he is objective that the combined
Protestant churches have been a bit more successful. These examples,
in combination with those mentioned above, illustrate that there are
few topics which are less likely to be dealt with in an accurate yet
penetrating manner than American Catholicism.

As for the distant future, the views which European thinkers express
on the destiny of the various forms of religion in the United States
may generally be broken down into two categories. On the one hand,
there are those that predict the substitution of some secular impulse
for religion in America, while on the other, there are those which
claim that religion will survive, but in some altered form. An observation representative of the former belief is Denis Brogan's interrogation

"what was to replace Him (God)? Could anything replace Him but "Democracy" made into an object of worship, or business, or success?" While the assumption that God is dead mirrors the agnosticism of the questioner, the theory that democracy is in the process of being elevated to a religion here is not peculiar to Brogan. In contrast, M. J. Bonn writes of a religious synthesis which would combine "the pagan joy of Greek life with the moral responsibility of Christianity." This is an interesting prediction, but it must be remembered that Christianity contains many Greek elements; at least a partial synthesis has long been effected. Hilaire Belloc likewise foresees the development of a new religion in this country, ("not an isolated, fractional experiment, but a great national or cultural invention") although Belloc foresees a clash with Catholicism which Bonn fails to mention.

One must leave an evaluation of these vague prophecies to a later generation, and instead close with a few words of summary regarding the contemporary religious scene. As has been pointed out in this chapter, European observers generally agree that Fundamentalism is decreasing in power in the United States, while most of them also recognize that the influence of Puritanism is on the decline. There is, however, considerable disagreement abroad as to whether religion *per se* is actually dying out in this country, despite the fact that a widespread belief exists in Europe that the religious impulse of this nation is not as profound as is that of Europe. But it must be remembered that the European religious scene is presently in a state of ferment, so that analysts there are perhaps in a poor position to evaluate American religion objectively. In any event, the material presented in this chapter gives little indication that Europeans are less free from religious prejudice than we are, and thus their generalizations should be regarded with caution.

CHAPTER XII

PRAGMATISM AND MATERIALISM

Despite the fact that European observers usually regard pragmatism and materialism as the representative philosophies of the twentieth century United States, various elements of both traditions were present here in varying degrees long before 1900. But prior to that date the technique of mass production had as yet been applied only on a moderate scale, so that American wealth had not yet reached the point where it was met by the charge that it was a manifestation of materialism. Likewise, a vernacular tradition was developing in this nation prior to the twentieth century, but pragmatism had as yet to find its exponents of genius who were to enshrine its tenets in memorable prose. For this reason, the following analysis of the pragmatic and materialist elements in American life is made with special reference to the last sixty years or so, since these two philosophies during this period have come to be regarded abroad as typical expressions of American civilization.

In his volume *The Opium of The Intellectuals* Raymond Aron observes that "the 'American way of life' is the negation of what the European intellectual means by the word ideology." Aron is, of course, referring here to the pragmatic tradition with its stress on results rather than on principles, an outlook which differs sharply from the idealist philosophy with its emphasis on ends rather than on means. Harold Laski points out with justification that pragmatism is not a uniquely American contribution to world civilization, but European thinkers more often criticize the American form of this philosophy on the grounds that it is not a formal system of thought. The same charge, however, has been levelled against that other significant modern philosophical movement, existentialism, which also is not without its past precedents. In regard to the non-systematic character of pragmatism, Geoffrey Gorer remarks that "in America there is a growing tendency to regard each aspect of the universe separately and discretely, as though each existed independently of the other." Gorer adds that the "American view of the world is the furthest removed ... from what can perhaps be called the primitive view of the (cosmos)," and it must be admitted that the primitive world view is highly systematic, in contrast to the pragmatic.

Some European thinkers (Bertrand Russell is a prominent example) do take the trouble to distinguish between pragmatism and instrumentalism, but instrumentalism is more often than not regarded as a variety of the pragmatic philosophy. Russell observes of instrumentalism that "there is no place in this outlook for the beatific vision nor for any notion of final excellence," but this evaluation could just as easily be applied to pragmatism. Another complicating factor is the surprisingly widespread tendency abroad to label the tradition of William James and John Dewey as utilitarianism, which certainly is not correct technically. As Frank Thistlethwaite points out, "Benthamisn (utilitarianism) had little direct influence on the United States."

In addition, the English brand of utilitarianism was conceived in reference to the pleasure and pain principle, and this is not a fundamental consideration in either pragmatism or instrumentalism. An examination of the remarks of European commentators on American "utilitarianism," however, reveals that this word is used more or less as a substitute for pragmatism (or instrumentalism) rather than as a term signifying a philosophical approach similar to but distinguishable from both. It is pointed out in the next chapter, moreover, that many foreign critics prefer to describe the Deweyian element in modern American education as utilitarian rather than as instrumental. This usage is, of course, questionable although it is quite widespread.

The observations of Europeans on American "utilitarianism" are, in fact, sometimes rather odd, as many of them are characterized by fancy rather than by insight. This is true even of the assertions of Hermann von Keyserling and German writer Robert Jungk. One must, for example, label as nonsensical von Keyserling's statement that in America "an artistic genius must deteriorate, all the more so, as he is the most wayward and sensitive of human types." Although the genius is frequently regarded as impractical, his message to society must have its practical consequences, or else he would not be finally recognized by his less gifted fellow man. Similarly, one must question Jungk's assertion that free will here should "be flatly classed as an unstable element and ruled out," as only determinism guarantees reliability. There are instances in which one is able to obtain results only through experimentation, and the use of the experimental method

implies a lack of certainty which is out of place in a philosophy based
on predestination.

On the other hand, Amaury de Riencourt is quite correct in his
observation that there does exist a certain degree of conflict between
the utilitarian and idealistic elements in American culture. Reinhold
Niebuhr has dealt with this point at length in his *The Irony of American History*. But in maintaining that "this fundamental schism is
another consequence of the atomistic outlook of the Reformation," de
Riencourt overlooks the fact that both philosophical attitudes date
back many centuries before this historic event. He also overempha-
sizes the unity of Western thought up to that time. However, one
should not judge the entire body of European comments on American
pragmatism on the basis of the remarks set forth here, as the majority of these assertions are sound and sane.

A point which those Europeans commentators who write on American pragmatism often stress is that an interest in abstraction is the
exception rather than the rule with most Americans. Luigi Barzini
observes, for example, that "theoretical thinking probably seems to
them (Americans) a shameful weakness, which they must hide at
all costs, as it sets them apart from their fellow countrymen." In
addition, Raymond Bruckberger affirms that there is an essential
difference between pragmatic and dialectical thinking. It is not
surprising, therefore, that many European analysts point out that
ideas *per se* are not worshipped here. Thus Harold Laski notes that
Americans tend to experiment in the realm of everyday things but not
in that of fundamental ideas, while M. J. Bonn adds that whatever ideas
are formulated here are meant to be executed as well as reasoned out.[63]
There may be an inherent danger in this widespread distrust of ideas,
as Jacques Maritain maintains, but this does not constitute proof
that Americans rely mainly on intuition rather than on intelligence, as
Hermann von Keyserling suggests. The fact is that Americans usually
do not deny the value of ideas, provided that these ideas have practical
consequences, and many European observers seem to have lost sight
of this point.

Certain other differences also exist between pragmatism and
idealism. Philip Gibbs notes one point of dissimilarity in his reference
to the American tendency to think in black and white terms, as this
phenomenon is a characteristic of idealism rather than of pragmatism.
The pragmatic world view, of course, conceives the universe in blurred
shades of gray, while the idealistic outlook often places reality in un-
naturally sharp focus. In addition, the concepts of time characteristic

of pragmatism and idealism differ. Simone de Beauvoir fancifully writes that the idealistic philosophy regards the past as "a thing embalmed," and the future as something which "can be deduced mechanically," while one might observe that the pragmatic tradition conceives time more as a process in which acts are being consummated. Lastly, Bernard Fay traces the American tendency to conform to idealism rather than pragmatism, and the systematic body of thought inherent in the former is admittedly more conducive to conformism than is a piece-meal and practical outlook. One might also argue that pragmatism leads to conformity, but only in the sense that it is a technique accepted by society as a whole.

The question of American materialism is one of the most controversial issues of the present epoch. One of the main findings of this volume is to expose as fallacious the assumption that European thinkers invariably maintain that Americans are materialists. Actually the majority of competent foreign commentators, from James Bryce to Hermann von Keyserling, strongly emphasize that such is not the case. Moreover, the minority who do claim that materialism runs rampant here usually base their conclusions on rather naive reasoning. They often argue, for example, that since the United States is the richest country in the world, it is therefore the most materialist, and they rarely present any new insights or ideas to support their position. On the other hand, those critics who deny that materialism is the rule here are generally much more subtle, and their observations thus require a more lengthy analysis.

But before examining the role of materialism in the history of this nation, it is necessary to determine where this philosophical tradition is located in relationship to the other ideologies predominant in American life, idealism and pragmatism. On the one hand, the materialist outlook resembles the idealistic (as well as the primitive) in that the universe is conceived in terms of a system, and as a result they stand in sharp contrast to pragmatism with its stress on the concrete and particular. In addition, both idealism and materialism possess a hierarchy of values, although that of the latter is an inversion of that of the former, while pragmatism does not. Yet despite certain similarities, idealism and materialism are often regarded as being incompatible, and it is likely that a materialist would be a pragmatist before he would be an idealist. This is because the pragmatic and materialist philosophies belong to different families, so that they are complementary more than they are contradictory. Nevertheless, some thinkers abroad do claim that materialism and idealism may be reconciled, and this point will be examined later in the chapter.

In criticizing the theory that America is materialist, James Bryce observed that in the United States "the race for wealth, not really greater than in Western Europe, is a passion rather for success in making than for the pleasure in enjoying a fortune."[54] A distinction obviously exists between the desire to become rich and the more praiseworthy urge to accomplish something, although William James once did make a rather unpleasant remark concerning American worship of the "bitch goddess Success." Bertrand Russell also maintains that the accusation that Americans are fonder of money than are Europeans is an unjust one; he claims that it is inspired by envy. Russell points out that the real reason why the aristocrats of European history were respected by the masses was that they were rich rather than because they possessed certain admirable qualities.

One might suggest in this connection that the mere detection of the presence of materialism in American life is not sufficient proof that this country is materialist, as it is also necessary to calculate its strength relative to that of idealism and pragmatism. Thus Raoul de Roussy de Sales asserts that America "should (not) have survived the innumerable assaults of piratical groups" if an idealistic belief in the principles of democracy had not taken precedence over the materialist impulse. Of course, Bryce, Russell, and de Roussy de Sales would probably not deny that materialism plays a role in American civilization. All three, however, imply that its significance is exaggerated, which is in no small part due to confused thinking as to what constitutes a materialist approach to life.

One of the most devastating indictments of those European writers who regard American society as materialist is the observation of Jacques Maritain that "in a number of my fellow Europeans the fable in question proceeds from an old prejudice, confusing spirituality with an aristocratic contempt for an improvement in material life." Moreover, there does exist an ascetic point of view among certain Christians which tends to correlate worldly failure with spiritual success. Maritain also points out that it may be true that materialism thrives in the industrial society of America, but that it prospers in other industrial areas all over the world as well. Maritain adds that although industrialism obviously is an important factor in American life, it is not the only one, as the people of the United States, being "pioneers and free men under God," are also idealists.

On the other hand, Hermann von Keyserling maintains that what is generally regarded as American materialism is in actuality the foundation of future spirituality, as "in the United States the outer form has run far ahead of its content—which happens always where it does not lag behind." This theory is doubtless related to the hypothesis that technological progress has outstripped spiritual growth in America. Von Keyserling also notes that one of the components of the so-called materialist civilization of this country is really spirituality in embryo form, while the other "is due to the senility of the over-aged eighteenth century type." Thus one is confronted with an amalgam of that which is dying and that which is being born, so that American culture is a composite of extremes rather than a mature unity.

It is quite difficult either to refute or prove such an imaginative explanation as that of von Keyserling, but quite a few other European writers agree with his theory that the material in America may eventually become the spiritual. Thus Raoul de Roussy de Sales remarks "that the concept of happiness and that of progress have been merged into one has had as a further consequence the nearly complete elimination of the opposition between the spiritual and the material." A similar belief is reflected in Andre Siegfried's assertion that "the American is an apostle, but one who speaks in terms of dollars about things of the spirit." Thus he is simultaneously an idealist and a materialist. Since both materialism and idealism are systems and possess a contradictory hierarchy of values, it would seem that some sort of a synthesis would be impossible, but it must be remembered that theologians have even attempted to reconcile good and evil.

Returning now to the anti-materialist line of thought, M. J. Bonn observes that the tendency to measure things in a quantitative manner here is often falsely interpreted abroad as a sign of materialism, and that moral appraisals are not usually based on such a quantitative scale of values in this country. Bonn also relates the emphasis on measuring in America to the growth of scientific techniques both in the United States and elsewhere, and it is admittedly true that without accurate measurements a highly developed science is an obvious impossibility. For this reason, one has to question the observation of Ernest Teilhac that a stress on statistics is an essentially American phenomenon,[55] for the statistical approach is in evidence everywhere throughout the civilized world. Indeed, it often appears that Europeans are of the opinion that quantitative and qualitative measurements are incompatible, and this theory reflects the most naive reasoning imaginable, despite its widespread acceptance.

It must be admitted that it is precisely this emphasis on quantity which those European thinkers who are eager to prove that Americans are materialists usually stress. Thus Salvador de Madariaga writes that "these American people worship a God which they have not troubled to name, but which is ever present in their thoughts and deeds." De Madariaga adds that "to us philosophers, it appears in the abstract form of Quantity." Richard Muller-Freienfels similarly asserts that "quantity, in America, is not a fact, as with us; it is a value"; quality, in short, is subordinated to a secondary role here. This chain of reasoning reflects the widespread European sentiment that Americans may excel in mass production, but Europeans surpass them in handicraft.

Also of significance is the relationship which Lewis Namier detects in America's dominant features between "their colossal size and their comparative uniformity." Many Europeans believe that the quantitative approach predominant in the United States encourages a striving towards the goal of immensity through its identification of bigness and value. On the other hand, they usually claim that Europeans place much more stress on individuality and originality than do Americans, as these two traits are more likely to develop in an environment in which quality predominates. Moreover, Simone de Beauvoir claims that a correlation exists here between quantity and temporality, as de Beauvoir finds that the relative unimportance of the qualitative standard is allied to a belief that things lack durability. One might infer on this basis that the presence of a quantitative standard in America is paralleled by the relative absence of tradition here, and this is one of the focal points of European criticisms of the United States.

In conclusion, it is ironic that the two philosophies which are generally regarded abroad as predominant in modern American life are as old as man, yet European observers nevertheless continue to analyze in volume after volume what most of them consider to be new and highly original philosophical approaches. Similarly, there are both pragmatic and materialist elements at work in the European civilization of today, but observers there often ignore their presence in their attempt to set up a false philosophical dichotomy between the Old World and the New. Differences obviously do exist between the American and European varieties of civilization, but certainly the philosophical dissimilarity is not as great as European analysts would

have one believe. The latter perhaps would be more convincing
if they tried to demonstrate that pragmatism and materialism were
slightly more prominent in American life than they are in European,
but it appears that the majority of commentators abroad do not
restrict themselves to making such a subtle distinction.

CHAPTER XIII

INTELLECTUAL LIFE — PRO AND CON

One of the most controversial aspects of American life is that of the quality of culture in the United States. The overall impression that one obtains from an examination of European thought is that American culture is looked upon in a rather condescending manner. Graham Wallas speaks for quite a number of other Europeans when he asserts that "America does not now 'pull its weight' in the boat of world-civilization." And it is often charged that the technical mastery so much in evidence in this country has not been accompanied by a genuine culture.

Indeed, it is frequently pointed out abroad that the United States has produced fewer geniuses of the first order in the last two centuries than has Europe. Thus Sigmund Freud, George Bernard Shaw, and Claude Debussy are ranked higher there than such possible American counterparts as William James, Walt Whitman, and George Gershwin.

It is also claimed at times on the other side of the Atlantic that the intellectual life of the United States is only a pale carbon copy of that of Europe. In this connection Wyndham Lewis writes that America "absorbs not only numbers of people from all the European and other countries, but also their ideas." Surprisingly, this nation has been challenged even as to the originality of its contributions in the various fields of science. Thus Geoffrey Gorer expresses a common belief when he maintains that Europeans make the original discoveries and Americans improve on these path-breaking findings.[56] In an era in which men like Robert Oppenheimer and Jonas Salk are stars of the first magnitude in the international scientific firmament, such an observation may seem a bit absurd. It should be remembered, however, that up to the last quarter century or so, one could probably count on the fingers of one hand the truly original scientists that this country produced (Benjamin Franklin, Willard Gibbs, and Joseph Henry). Moreover, American failures in the satellite race cannot be disregarded.

This supposed lack of culture in America, or the poor quality thereof, has been attributed to various factors by European commentators. The most common of these is the belief that the general atmosphere of this country is not conducive to the development of a high cultural level. As far as specific pinpointing is concerned, Arnold Toynbee observes that the middle class of this nation "had gone farthest down the *descensus Averni* which Rome had foreboded." Andre Siegfried, on the other hand, places the blame for the low state of American culture on the fact that "west of the Alleghanies at any rate, there is no intellectual aristocracy capable of thinking for itself and courageously opposing the masses." In broader terms, Lucien Romier explains this cultural deficiency on the grounds that creativity is distrusted in America because it is to a large degree experimental. According to Romier, the artist is not in harmony with the philosophy of success predominant in the United States because he does not absolutely guarantee results. Although these judgments are perceptive one hesitates to accept them as totally accurate.

As might be expected, the so-called mass culture of America is the focal point for criticisms abroad. Many European authors frequently throw all restraint to the winds in dealing with its various manifestations, and most of them regard Hollywood as its epitome. One, in fact, often encounters such diatribes as the remark of Harold Laski that "Hollywood is a mass of unfathomable contradictions, where men who know nothing of anything act upon the assumption of their omniscience." George Duhamel is similarly of the view that "any people subject for half a century to the actual influence of the American 'movie' is on the way to the worst decadence." Even radio and television are on the receiving end of some of this abuse, although they on occasion do feature programs which cater to the intellectual. Thus Salvador de Madariaga speaks of the lowbrow entertainment provided by the American radio industry, while Frank Thistlethwaite characterizes American video in terms of Liberace, Westerns, and give-away programs. There seems to be a general feeling in Europe that any communications medium which serves a large public is culturally bankrupt, and doubtless this view is tied in with the widespread European assumption that quantity and quality are not compatible.

In regard to American reading habits, the newspaper usually is cited abroad as a symbol of inferior culture and vulgar taste. H. A. L. Fisher regards its often formidable size as evidence that it caters to advertisements rather than to knowledge, while Odette Keun believes that its readers are often "ignorant and silly people." James Bryce, who is also somewhat disenchanted with the American press, asserts that the people let the newspapers do their thinking for them, and as a result the press is more of an effective force in shaping public opinion in the United States than it is anywhere else. Although they do not say so, these European critics apparently believe that newspapers should be fountains of immortal prose rather than vehicles for the dissemination of information, and this theory is not shaken by the fact that their own newspapers are largely functional in nature.

Jazz is one American cultural phenomenon which one might expect to be an object of favorable comment in Europe, since this art form now has become a fixture among European intellectuals. However, the reaction towards it is rather mixed, in that it has been criticized as well as praised abroad. American jazz has been attacked even by a thinker of the stature of Jean-Paul Sartre, who writes that it is only "capable of limited development and (is) in process of slow decline." George Duhamel, moreover, describes it as "a triumph of barbaric folly." As was pointed out earlier, Arnold Toynbee regards the introduction of a primitive element (which Toynbee regards jazz to be) into an advanced civilization as a sign of decay, and quite obviously other European analysts are of a similar opinion. It is ironical indeed that American civilization is often accused of being both non-organic and non-spontaneous by foreign writers, while one of the few natural art forms it has produced is widely regarded as a token of decadence. This is only one of many inconsistencies in European thought concerning the United States.

Not every commentator would agree with the general tenor of the opinions analyzed thus far in this chapter, but those who praise American culture extravagently are probably in a minority. One such exception is Hilaire Belloc, who bluntly asserts that "the United States are not merely an enlargement of our European culture, still less a mere branch of it." Few critics venture to claim that the products of the American cultural tradition have always been original; most European writers (including Harold Laski) have set 1914 as the date on which America first began to break with European culture. On the other hand, Halvdan Koht goes back to the early nineteenth century in his claim that American inventions inaugurated the "Americanization" of Europe, but Koht may be dismissed from this discussion, as he speaks in terms of technology rather than art.

Returning to the twentieth century, at least a few distinguished European critics claim the United States is evolving an independent culture today. For example, Andre Maurois concedes that "it is impossible not to admire the prodigious effort which has been made by

America, during the last forty years, to give itself an artistic culture."
Raymond Bruckberger also expresses admiration for American creators;
he lists Robert Oppenheimer, William Faulkner, and John J.
Becker (a composer) among the leaders of this country's intellectual
surge. If one is to reconcile the charge that America lacks culture
with the view expressed here, apparently the only way to accomplish
this feat is to conclude that both opinions are valid, but that each
applies only to a particular period of United States history.

As far as the specific contributions of the United States to world
culture are concerned, it is perhaps in the field of philosophy that
American creativity has been most widely praised abroad. As Bertrand Russell writes, "to my mind the best work that has been done
anywhere in philosophy ... during the present century has been
done in America." Moreover, the American philosophical tradition
is invariably identified in Europe with pragmatism and instrumentalism, and European analysts consider John Dewey even more than
William James as *the* American philosopher. Such important
thinkers as Russell and Hermann von Keyserling recognize the pre-
eminence of Dewey, and Amaury de Riencourt regards the founder
of instrumentalism as the symbol of American civilization.

On the other hand, George Santayana is rarely mentioned by European critics and scholars as a representative American thinker, a neglect traceable to his birth in Spain and, even more important, to the
fact that his atheistic piety and naturalistic materialism are far removed from the tradition of James and Dewey. But despite the
stature that Dewey and to a lesser extent James have attained in
Europe, it must be admitted that their fame is not primarily attributable to their individual genius. A much more important consideration is that Europeans generally consider the philosophical tradition which Dewey and James represent as not only the most important intellectual movement in the modern United States, but also as a
thought process characteristic of the American way of life in general.

American literature is likewise widely recognized by Europeans
as being of importance, but agreement as to its quality is not as
complete as in the field of philosophy. Despite the fact that Richard
Muller-Freienfels describes Walt Whitman as "the most significant
representative whom America has yet produced in the field of art,"
many European critics believe that one must look to the more
modern period for a truly original American literature. Thus Denis
Brogan notes that as of 1949 there were three living American Nobel
Prize winners in the field of literature and none from England, while

H. G. Wells singles out Sherwood Anderson, Sinclair Lewis, and Theodore Dreiser as American writers worthy of special praise.

In regard to attitudes towards life reflected in our literature, Andre Maurois represents a widespread European sentiment in his claim that it is characterized by realism and naturalism, and adds that modern American writing represents "a reaction against complacent optimism, against puritanism, and against sentimentalism." This seems to be a cogent evaluation of the trend in recent years. On the other hand, John St. Loe Strachey accuses the contemporary literature of this nation of being chaotic. This condition, however, is probably due more to the diversity characteristic of modern writing in general than to a lack of direction here.

American contributions to history, economics, music, and art perhaps have been discussed less extensively by European writers. As a result, each will be summarized here in terms of a few key individuals, together with some remarks on why these particular personages command so much respect on the other side of the Atlantic. In the discipline of history, Charles A. Beard and Frederick Jackson Turner are probably the most publicized figures, although Beard's economic determinism is doubtless more congenial to the Marxian indoctrinated European mind than is Turner's frontier thesis. Much admiration also has been expressed for the liberal literary historian Vernon Parrington. The lone figure of Thorstein Veblen stands out in economics, perhaps because his critical approach to American society is shared by many Europeans. Veblen, in fact, has pushed into relative obscurity such important but less flamboyant American economists as Wesley C. Mitchell. Over the years Veblen's European fame has seemingly increased rather than declined.

George Gershwin similarly towers over other American composers of serious music in the judgment of most foreign critics, but Gershwin's eminence should be attributed as much to his popular songs as to his longer classical compositions. In addition, Aaron Copland and the once-neglected Charles Ives are highly regarded abroad. From the point of view of art, James McNeill Whistler is generally accepted as an important figure, chiefly because of his influence on European painting. On the other hand, the creations of such controversial abstract expressionists as Jackson Pollock have obtained a rather mixed reaction from European commentators. Of course, numerous other individuals in the above fields and related ones might be mentioned (such as Frank Lloyd Wright in architecture), but limitations of space hinders the listing of more than a critical sampling of these path-breaking creators.

Having examined the question of whether or not a high level of culture exists in the United States, let us now turn to an examination of attitudes regarding the role of the intellectual in American life. Generally speaking, an impression exists abroad that the intellectual does not fare as well in the United States as he does in Europe. Thus Raymond Aron notes that American society does not persecute its intellectuals as a rule, but that indifference may be a worse burden for them to bear than persecution. The belief that artists are not appreciated in this country is also widespread, and Jacques Maritain is quite displeased because "their opinions carry less weight than that of prominent business men."[57] Ludwig von Mises similarly points out that a gulf exists between the business man and the intellectual in America, as American intellectuals have a greater anti-capitalist bias than have their European brethren. (This, however, is a debatable claim). It must be admitted, nevertheless, that a schism does exist in America between the business man's highly commercialized approach to art and the artist's concept of art for art's sake. This lack of rapport is exaggerated by the belief which the business man holds that the true test of a product is its marketability rather than its quality.

The artist or thinker may, of course, be influenced by American society more than he cares to admit. Raymond Aron notes that the typical member of the American intelligentsia is an expert, as specialization is a key feature of the system of mass production which has been evolved in this country. In general, nevertheless, it must be admitted that the true American intellectual is no more a narrow specialist than is his European counterpart, and a certain contempt for the technician is often found in intellectual circles in the United States. But despite the criticisms of the inadequate role that the intellectual plays in shaping public policy here, many European writers have come to the conclusion that he is now assuming a more important position in American life. Harold Laski attributes this gain in prestige to the fact that "the intellectuals themselves realize increasingly the futility of a theory divorced from action"; they accordingly have come down from their so-called ivory towers into the realities of everyday life. Laski's observation is admittedly a valid one, for many American intellectuals have come to recognize in recent years that they have an obligation to society, and that they should do something positive instead of lamenting the fact that society does not appreciate them.

It is appropriate that a review of American education should follow a discussion of American culture; European intellectuals have often evaluated the former in the same adverse manner as they have the latter. A typical expression of the belief that the educational system of this country is deficient is the observation of Harold Laski that "American education has not met the challenge with a success proportionate to its intensity." Moreover, many other analysts abroad share Laski's belief that the whole of American education is less than the sum of its parts. The more critical European commentators often maintain that the mere presence of the proper ingredients for a successful educational system is not enough unless a synthesis of these elements is effected, and they frequently question whether such a fusion has been brought about here.

A common trans-Atlantic sentiment is reflected in Philip Gibbs' remark that "university education in the (United) States does not go so deep or so high as our own." Here again is evidence of the stereotyped European belief that Europe represents quality and America quantity. Although Gibbs does admit that the sharing of numerous young Americans in the university experience has "raised the tone of the social code" of the United States, this in no way negates his essential argument. While Gibbs finds that the student has been the recipient of a superficial education, Bernard Fay believes that the teachers in American schools are the victims of a corresponding lack of prestige. Fay notes that for many decades the more outstanding students went into business rather than into teaching, and this judgment is substantiated by the facts.

On the other hand, Simone de Beauvoir charges that "most of the universities are cut off from literary and artistic *avant garde* movements," and that they are not providing "the spark which will stimulate doubt and a sense of responsibility in the young people." This remark is doubtless based on the fact that radical and revolutionary movements have not been tied to the universities here to the degree that they have been in Europe, but it ignores the fact that quite a few American universities have made an attempt to promote contemporary music, literature, and art. Graham Wallas, unlike de Beauvoir, tends to place the blame more on the students for this supposed lack of an intellectual ferment, as he writes that the young people here do not exert themselves enough. Wallas adds that it is necessary to replace impulse with purpose. This, however, is another stereotyped fallacy that is not borne out by the facts, as American students studying abroad have often shown that they are the equal of their European counterparts or even superior to them.

The financial aspects of American education also have been critically discussed by European analysts. Donations or grants have admittedly been used on occasion as a means of influencing educational policy, while the unequal distribution of funds within the school system has resulted in educational standards of uneven quality. Thus Harold Laski complains that "American universities have suffered, for at any rate half a century, from the excessive domination of wealth over their activities." On the other hand, Andre Maurois attributes the unequal school facilities in various states to the fact that some are wealthier and have more money to spend than others. The first of these assertions is something of a cliche, as it has been stressed in such books as Thorstein Veblen's *The Higher Learning in America*. The second is more justified, as H. G. Wells and many other European writers have pointed out that Southern schools, for example, are generally inferior. Moreover, it would seem that the only solution to this problem of financial inequality is some form of governmental control over the entire school system. Anti-statist commentators, however, often charge that this expedient might result in the creation of a situation as bad as the one that Laski envisages, only in this case the schools would be pawns of Washington instead of Wall Street.

It is indeed ironic that Europeans frequently maintain that it would be desirable for American educational facilities to be more uniform, as many intellectuals abroad violently attack American life on the grounds that it lacks the variety which is supposedly found in Europe. In fact, many European critics charge that the American educational system is over-standardized; they often claim that this over-standardization is due largely to the introduction of certain mass production techniques into the educational process. As for education specialization (or over-specialization), one might note Harold Laski's criticism of the Ph. D. degree that "in place of the thinker, it puts the card index," while "in place of the play of ideas, it puts the footnote and the bibliography." This observation focuses on one very important danger of the application of assembly line methods to doctoral research, and it noteworthy that Jacques Barzun has suggested that more weight be placed on the M. A. degree by universities.

Probably the most important adverse judgment which European analysts level against American education is that it is not an education in the sense that certain cultural values are transmitted. Instead, they charge that it is utilitarian, since it is frequently geared to preparing the student for vocational success. The ideas of William James and particularly John Dewey, of course, have influenced American education to a considerable degree, and it is on this very point that European commentators perhaps most severely criticize the effect of pragmatism and instrumentalism on American life. Thus Odette Keun charges that "primarily the school is viewed as the instrument with which you fashion your future career,"[58] while J. A. Spender complains that the predominance of utilitarian techniques suffocates the insatiable curiosity of the student. A longer period of time is probably necessary for a proper evaluation of whether the position represented by John Dewey or the classical approach of Robert Hutchins is right, but it should be remembered that the utilitarian approach to education did not develop in a vacuum. The Deweyian philosophy, of course, was evolved as a result of certain deficiences in the classical approach, and it must be admitted in all fairness that an education which does not look to the future as well as to the past is only a halfway education.

Various commentators abroad do tend to be quite laudatory in their remarks concerning American education, but they are probably outnumbered by the critics. John St. Loe Strachey, for example, observes that "if I were to be asked what...I think the greatest thing in modern America, I should say without hesitation—the splendid and growing manifestation of the University spirit." This remark, however, would not be received with much sympathy in Europe, as Strachey also praises the utilitarian features of the American educational system. Alfred Zimmern similarly speaks of "the golden quality of the American undergraduate," while Philip Guedalla is quite enthusiastic in his reference to Eastern universities, but the commendations of the friends of American education are generally not as vigorous as are the criticisms of its foes. It appears, moreover, that those European commentators who attack the American educational system generally do so because the American or utilitarian approach to education differs from the European or classical one. On the other hand, those writers abroad who do praise the educational system of this nation (Strachey and a few other excepted) often do so only to the extent that American schools fulfill the European concept of education. At best, Americans approach but never reach the European ideal, and for this reason the American who expects European analysts to laud American education excessively is likely to be disappointed.

Regardless of what they may think of American education as a whole, European observers often express admiration for certain aspects of the educational system of this country. These praiseworthy features, moreover, are usually the ones to which American educators also point with pride. From the comparative point of view, Americans enjoy more academic freedom than do Europeans, while a larger proportion of young people attend college in the United States than in Europe. In addition, certain American schools (Duke, for example) have been lavishly endowed by wealthy benefactors, and the facilities (especially for scientific work) of some large universities surpass anything that Europe has to offer. Accordingly, the credit side of the balance sheet of American education is not totally blank, regardless of the items that might be listed in the debit column, and few European commentators are so biased that they will not admit this.

If one attempts to generalize about intellectual life in the United States, he is confronted with a situation in which the observations pertinent to one branch (education) are frequently not applicable to the other one (culture). The reason for this is that the charge of utilitarianism which thinkers abroad at times direct against American education is not as often levelled against American culture. This is because European analysts usually criticize American creators for imitating European culture, which as a rule is non-utilitarian, rather than for being original. Consequently, it might be noted that American education is attacked abroad because it is not European, while American culture is assaulted because it is not American. Such a dichotomy between education and culture is alien to the European scene, moreover, as a somewhat closer relationship exists between the two than it does in the United States. In addition, many European observers maintain that education in America is rooted too far in the future, while culture is grounded too deeply in the past. Thus as is frequently the case, Europe represents to many Europeans a golden mean between the extremes which they believe to be characteristic of American life.

Chapter XIV

THE ATLANTIC COMMUNITY MOVES APART

A comprehensive examination of various European attitudes toward the relationship which exists between the Old World and the New serves as an effective prelude to the concluding chapter. Although America and Europe have been analyzed in conjunction at times throughout this volume, they were not so treated in a systematic manner previously. The first part of this chapter, however, is concerned with individual European nations and their rapport or lack thereof vis-a-vis the United States. Here Great Britain logically is accorded the most space, with France being covered more briefly, while Germany and the other European countries are dealt with in an incidental manner. The second section is much more far-reaching in scope, as the question of whether Europe and America are basically similar or dissimilar will be examined, and it is hoped, resolved at least partially.

In regard to England, many European analysts believe that there exists a considerable degree of friction between Great Britain and the United States, and they attribute this lack of rapport to a number of factors. One very significant point is made by Denis Brogan, who writes that most Britishers are ignorant of American history,[59] and that the English think that the schools of this country place Great Britain in an uncomplimentary position historically. It might be added, however, that an attempt has been made in recent years to remedy this deficiency, as prominent historians of both nations have made guest appearances in the other country. But this state of antagonism should not be attributed entirely to inadequate knowledge, for there appear to be certain intrinsic differences between America and England which cause distrust and resentment.

For example, the Britisher is often regarded as affected by Americans because he speaks with an accent, a phenomenon which has been noted by Bertrand Russell and many other European writers. In addition, the representation that America is especially virtuous is resented in Great Britain,[60] while the widespread English sentiment that the United States is an extension of England is viewed with distaste in this country. The accumulation of such seemingly minor grievances has resulted in a mutual hostility, albeit of limited proportions. It also might be mentioned that Americans probably receive British criticisms of the United States with more displeasure than they greet those coming from any other European nation, for as J. A. Spender writes, "there is never a clean sheet in the account with the British." Likewise, American barbs are usually greeted with clinched teeth in Great Britain; the English appear to be surprisingly sensitive to American criticisms.

Various differences between Great Britain and the United States are also emphasized by Frank Thistlethwaite. In referring to England as "the Citadel", Thistlethwaite remarks that it is "a society of guardians protecting a crossroads of traffic." On the other hand, Thistlethwaite regards the United States as "the Caravan," since it is "a society of traders committed to the journey." In regard to specific dissimilarities, Andre Maurois notes that in Great Britain political parties have tended to be ideological, while in the United States they have inclined to be administrative. As R. H. S. Crossman also points out, party loyalty is much stronger in England than it is in America. Another significant point of contrast is that the historical consciousness of the Englishman is much more highly developed than is that of the American. Thus Lewis Namier observes that the average Englishman thinks in terms of a past extending back a millenium, while most Americans hardly ever cast a retrospective glance.

European critics also have noticed a contrast in social behavior between the inhabitants of the two nations. In regard to this difference, Bertrand Russell writes that Americans are much more likely to express their emotions publicly than are the English, as a result of which Americans may be alternately affectionate or brutal. Russell also suggests that the English "may miss the caresses, but you (Americans) also miss the blows." Finally, one might cite Frank Thistlethwaite's observation that in England the political and professional occupations possess the greatest prestige, while in the United States the economic ones rank the highest. It is probably true that profit has generally been regarded with greater social approval in America than it has in Great Britain, and this is obviously one reason why some European thinkers have claimed that the United States is materialist.

An examination of the history of the last two centuries reveals, however, that the relationship of America and England has not been static, but rather has been in a constant state of flux. There undoubtedly are commentators abroad who would object to the treatment of American history as a branch of that of the English-speaking peoples in general, a technique, for example, which is characteristic of the writings of James Bryce. On the other hand, it must be recognized that relations have been more intimate between this nation and Great Britain than they have between America and any other European country. A few European critics, including Hilaire Belloc, do claim that England was somewhat hostile towards the United States up to the 1860's, but this belief is not entirely accurate. In fact, nineteenth century British radicals felt a certain rapport with the democratic experiments of the New World, as was noted in the seventh chapter.

Moreover, pre-1900 America and England resembled each other in that isolationism played a key role in the foreign policy of both nations.[61] Likewise, as Arnold Toynbee points out, a *fin de siècle* confidence in the future was widespread in both countries during the last decade or so of the nineteenth century. In regard to the period since 1900, the most striking feature of the interplay of ideas between England and the United States is that it is now the British conservatives rather than the liberals who look to America for encouragement. Thus the claim of Frank Thistlethwaite that modern English reform has not been markedly influenced by American examples is quite justified, especially since the program of Lloyd George antedated that of Franklin Roosevelt by a quarter of a century.

However, there are also forces at work which tend to draw Great Britain and the United States closer together. In the first place, this nation and England are confronted by many difficulties of a related nature. Thus Lewis Namier writes that "the problems ... of government by representative assemblies and plebiscitarian autocracy in the person of Prime Minister or President, of direct popular government and government through organized parties, are very much alike in both countries." Secondly, the British Commonwealth is now in the process of evolution, and English authors (Norman Angell, for instance) often suggest ways in which the Commonwealth may be strengthened by imitating various principles of American federalism. Finally, a strong tie currently exists between American and British capitalists. Such left-wing European thinkers as G. D. H. Cole constantly lament this relationship in that it makes the position of the socialists more difficult, but it must be remembered that socialism is just as much an international movement as is capitalism.

In the case of France one also finds diverse reactions abroad as to the relationship which exists between that nation and the United

States. However, the overall impression one obtains is that a wider gap exists between France and America than between England and the United States. But this is only logical, since there is a language barrier between the two countries, as well as for many other reasons, such as that the impact of Catholicism has been much greater on France than it has been on America. In regard to this schism, Raymond Aron writes that "the technological civilization of the United States, with its ceaseless movement, its consuming desire to produce, to innovate, to break all records of quantity and productivity, is ... removed from French civilization, which is attempting to maintain modern industry within the framework of old institutions." Of course, America is not the embodiment of technology and France the incarnation of culture, but America probably stresses technology more than France does, while France apparently emphasizes culture to a greater degree.

For another analysis of this dichotomy, one might turn to Bernard Fay's remarks contrasting the French and American temperaments. Fay writes in this connection that "what seems to America dignity, France calls stubbornness or heaviness," and "what France considers witty, America often finds flippant and impertinent." For this reason, it is not surprising that Fay concludes that the masses of these two countries have never really understood each other, despite certain common traits such as a sincere zest for life and a deep idealism. It is obvious, moreover, that many distortions are present in the image which each nation holds of the other. As Andre Lafond points out, possibly the most mistaken impression that Americans have of France is that the latter is a land of pleasure and debauchery, although Lafond does admit the French often have encouraged the spreading of this false belief. On the other hand, one of the most flagrant French misconceptions about the United States is that cultural and spiritual values are not fully appreciated here. This opinion is doubtless rooted in what the French regard as a failure on our part to compliment them sufficiently for possessing those qualities which they believe to be characteristic of themselves.[62]

Numerous other differences are in evidence between France and America, and some of these merit analysis. Here one might mention Andre Tardieu's remark that "in the United States the individual seeks company," while "in France the individual seeks isolation," as this reflects the widespread European belief that American life is mass life. Despite this, however, the American is probably better off in regard to personal liberty than is the Frenchman, and even Tardiau admits that the nation is given priority over the individual in France, while it is subordinated to the latter here. Denis Brogan points out in this connection that the concept of the citizen is less legally concrete in France than it is in America. As for democracy, Bernard Fay theorizes that public opinion governs foreign policy in the United States much more than it does in France.[63] This statement, of course, is somewhat debatable, but many observers would maintain that such is the case with domestic policy as well.

It is true that France and America exerted a strong influence on each other at the time of the American and French Revolutions, and so distinguished a writer as Raymond Aron even regards this impact as profound. Nevertheless, there has not been continual political co-operation between the United States and France since then, and as Andre Tardieu observes, those two countries "have never made a combined effort that was not followed by immediate rupture." Likewise, the Physiocratic branch of the French economic tradition once influenced the thinking of this nation to a considerable degree, although Ernest Teilhac points out that other economic theories have now largely superseded it. In fact, as Andre Tardieu again suggests, economic issues have probably played a more important role in American than in French history.[64] Yet it would be a great mistake to maintain that France and the United States have not affected each other at all since 1800, for there has been a considerable artistic and literary interchange between the two countries. Bernard Fay thus notes that "Poe and Whitman gave to European literature an original impetus, when Hugo and Zola caused new movements of thought in the New World." But in general it must be admitted that it is only in the cultural field that Franco-American relations approach those of the Anglo-American community of interests.

As far as Germany and the other countries of Europe are concerned, the observations which European critics make on their relationship vis-a-vis the United States are so scattered and fragmentary that there is not much point in attempting any systematic analysis of them. There appears to be no other course of procedure open than to refer briefly to a few of the more interesting ones and then to pass on. In the case of Germany, one might mention Hermann von Keyserling's comments contrasting the German and American national characters, and Andre Siegfried's remarks differentiating the German and American concepts of the state. As for similarities, Arnold Toynbee's comparison of the American Civil War and the Bismarckian wars is especially perceptive. These observations, however, should be consulted individually for their unique insights rather than taken collectively as reflections of a climate of opinion.

One does occasionally unearth a significant observation on the ties which exist between the United States and the other nations of Europe, such as Alfred Zimmern's statement that the Swiss are the only European people who are really capable of understanding America. For the most part, however, European commentators usually deal with such relatively unimportant topics as the influence of the American Constitution on the Norwegian one of 1814[65] or the varying relationship between political parties and social classes in the United States and Sweden. Of course, a favorite conversation piece abroad is the similarities which supposedly exist between America and Rome, as these are stressed by Arnold Toynbee, Amaury de Riencourt, and quite a few other European analysts of note. But it must be recalled that this comparison is made with reference to the Rome of Caesar rather than to that of Mussolini. Although such an important European writer as Bertrand Russell does establish a relationship between ancient Athens and modern America, the usual tie which European thinkers emphasize is the one between the Greece of two and a half millenia ago and the Europe of today.

This set of parallels between the United States and Rome on the one hand and Europe and Greece on the other serves as a fitting introduction to the final half of this chapter, which is an examination of the relative degree of rapport which exists between the Old World and the New. In beginning, it might be noted that one of the most fascinating aspects of modern European thought on this nation is the analogies which European analysts frequently establish between the leading historical figures of the United States and those of Europe. Washington and de Gaulle, Hamilton and Disraeli, Lincoln and Bismarck, Rockefeller and Bismarck, Bryan and Hitler, and McCarthy and Hitler are a few of these combinations, some of which are quite perceptive. Such pairings, of course, are not always complimentary, but they show that similar historical figures have arisen in the Old World and the New; this point is often made by European commentators who claim that the civilizations of the two are similar.

Since both Arnold Toynbee and Oswald Spengler regard the United States and Europe as branches of a larger entity entitled Western Civilization, it is to be expected that they would compare rather than contrast the two. Spengler, for example, writes of "a last spiritual crisis that will involve all Europe and America," a remark which reflects the biological determinism so characteristic of the author of

THE ATLANTIC COMMUNITY MOVES APART

The Decline of the West. From a similarly pessimistic viewpoint, Harold Laski remarks that the same decay of traditional values is evident in the United States as in Europe. Thus Laski and Spengler add their voices to the chorus of Cassandras predicting a union of America and Europe in death. A slightly different approach is offered by Amaury de Riencourt, who suggests that "there is not a single criticism that can be levelled at America today that could not be levelled ten times over at most European nations—cheapness, lack of culture and refinement, vulgarity." On the other hand, Bernard Fay observes that this country serves as a magnifying glass for Europe, especially in regard to its faults, crimes, bad habits, and vices. While both of these observations are based on the less desirable features of American and European life, they exhibit a strong disagreement as to whether the United States has influenced Europe more than Europe has affected America.

In his book *American Themes* Denis Brogan makes the significant assertion that "the overflow of Europe from the sixteenth century on is the dominating theme of world history." Brogan, moreover, also notes that "the most striking and important example of the overflow is the United States." This view is a typical expression of the belief that the United States is essentially a European colony, as is the remark of Bertrand Russell that "the culture of America is closely akin to our own, and adaptation can be easy and painless." Such a theory would, of course, meet with widespread acceptance if it were applied to the early period of American history. But many American critics would question its present applicability, as they often stress our growing spiritual independence from Europe, as well as charging that the Old World is now imitating the New.

Nevertheless, quite a few European commentators maintain that the United States is actually moving closer to Europe. In writing of this impending union, Arnold Toynbee suggests that it is the result of the closing of the American West, and Toynbee adds that it would have taken place even if there had been no world wars. Toynbee also observes that this country is in the process of converting from a dynamic state to a static one, and it consequently is becoming more and more like Europe. This last theory is highly debatable; there exists neither widespread agreement nor conclusive proof that this nation is losing its dynamism. But Toynbee is not alone in his belief that the gap between the Old World and the New is narrowing; M. J. Bonn also detects a growing dependence of America on Europe. Bonn correlates this Europeanization of the United States with the end of the colonial phase of American history. He contends that "thereby America has, from a social standpoint, become in some degree Europeanized." On the other hand, Bonn's observation that this nation is becoming capitalistic is rather puzzling; he offers no satisfactory explanation for this rather curious remark.

Although Jose Ortega y Gasset points out that "Europe has not been Americanized," and that "it has received no great influence from America," quite a few analysts abroad maintain that the impact of this nation on Europe has been as great, if not greater, than that of Europe on the United States. Lucien Romier writes in this connection that the financial ties between the Old World and the New are quite strong, but that "it is in the evolution of morals and tastes that American influence is most perceptible."[66] On the other hand, Guglielmo Ferrero, whose catalogue of influences is more extensive than that of Romier, refers to such American phenomena which have effected Europe as the emancipation of women, the growth of urban life, and the democratization of luxury. Innumerable similar remarks might also be noted; what is striking about many of them is that they stress that the impact of the U.S. on Europe has not been only technological, but also cultural. As for the future, one might note the prediction of Geoffrey Barraclough that later in this century or early in the next one Europe is destined to become an economic colony of the United States. This prophecy may seem a bit extreme, but many Europeans have voiced similar sentiments.

In regard to the theory that the relationship between the United States and Europe is essentially one of contrast, one encounters a mass of material which is both more extensive and more diverse than that supporting the opposing view. Moreover, this body of writing leads one to believe that the old stereotype of the United States as a pale carbon copy of Europe is no longer valid. One of the leading proponents of dissimilarity is Andre Siegfried, who notes in his *America Comes of Age* that "the old European civilization did not really cross the Atlantic, for the American re-awakening is not, as is generally supposed, simply a matter of degrees and dimensions."

Siegfried also refers to the different scales of values in the Old World and the New (qualitative vs. quantitative); he notes that there are important geographical, political, and psychological distinctions as well. J. A. Spender sums up Siegfried's remarks most succinctly in his observation that "the United States is making a characteristically American civilization in American surroundings." In addition, there are other writers abroad (such as Fritz Sternberg who visualize

Europe as a third force between America and Russia; this view is based on the assumption that there do exist certain fundamental dissimilarities between the Old World and the New.

As for the date on which America and Europe irrevocably moved apart, 1914 is the one which appears to be the favorite of many European commentators. Although M. J. Bonn prefers to emphasize this date as signalling American economic independence, many other Europeans tend to draw more extensive implications in regard to it. Thus Amaury de Riencourt remarks that "America became fully conscious of her own individuality during World War I." Although de Riencourt does admit that the closing of the American frontier, the limitations on immigration into this nation, and the decline of individualism in the United States were important elements in this break with Europe, he also observes that "it took the momentous shock of a global war to start an entirely new phase of America's evolution." But there are some Europeans who prefer to push this date a bit further back into history. For example, Lucien Romier asserts that America began to break away from Europe around the turn of the twentieth century; this theory modifies the 1914 hypothesis rather than rejects it. One might make the generalization that the United States gained its spiritual independence sometime between "Venezuela and Versailles" (i.e., 1895 and 1919) with the expectation that most critics abroad will accept it as valid.

Once it is admitted that the United States and Europe are dissimilar, the question is raised as to specific differences. The following analysis begins with an investigation of the political dissimilarities, as divergences are often detected in this field. Raoul de Roussy de Sales writes in this connection that in Europe political consciousness is an aspect of one's nationality, while in America it preceded American independence, which indicates that the political impulse is more vital in this country than it is abroad. It is difficult either to prove or disprove his theory, although it appears to be quite logical. But on the other hand, as Andre Siegfried points out, Americans do not question their basic institutions (the Constitution, etc.) to the extent that Europeans do. Consequently, one might observe that even if Americans are more politically active than are Europeans, they exert themselves on behalf of less important causes than do their trans-Atlantic counterparts.

As far as other political differences are concerned, Denis Brogan suggests that the political machine is an essentially American institution rather than a European one, and Ludwig von Mises observes that the concept of an *Obrigkeit* ("a government the authority of which is not derived from the people") is more characteristic of Europe than of the United States. Alfred Zimmern similarly asserts that political centralization is more predominant in the Old World than in the New, while Gunnar Myrdal declares that social engineering has not reached the stage in America that it has in Europe. Taken in conjunction, these half dozen points of contrast constitute a rather substantial defense of the theory that the United States and Europe are politically divergent, although many of the arguments expressed in other fields are just as convincing.

The economic dissimilarities between the Old World and the New are also emphasized. Fritz Sternberg declares that the tendency towards economic self-sufficiency is more pronounced here than in Europe, while G. D. H. Cole maintains that capitalism is still developing in America although it is currently dying in Europe. Cole's hypothesis is mirrored in the observation of Sternberg that the American form of free enterprise is not today feasible in the Old World. Significantly, the existence of a "single market" is the feature of the American economic system which European analysts probably stress the most in comparing the Old World with the New. As Gunnar Myrdal [67] and others note, the absence of internal tariffs and trade barriers gives the United States an almost unprecedented opportunity for economic development, and this is an advantage which Europe unfortunately lacks.

However, an awareness that the American economy is in many ways superior to those of Europe has not blunted the pens of critics. Thus Andre Siegfried suggests that Europe surpasses the United States in the production of specialized articles, while Richard Muller-Freienfels declares that mass production techniques are the servant in the Old World but the master in the New. These two negative judgments are widely stressed by other European writers as well. On the other hand, Odette Keun obviously expresses a minority viewpoint in her claim that Scandinavia, Holland, Switzerland, and to a lesser degree, England and France, have developed a better form of capitalist democracy than the United States.

Numerous other points of contrast between America and Europe which European observers stress might also be mentioned, but it is only practical to analyze a half dozen of them here. One very significant dissimilarity is noted by Barbara Ward, who suggests that the United States rather than Europe is now "the old familiar and stable world." This perceptive remark was obviously prompted by the upheavals that took place in Europe as the result of the two world wars. On the other hand, Frank Thistlethwaite writes that the American concept of nationality differs from the European in that it constitutes "not membership in a nation state, but in a voluntary society of people who chose to belong to it." Thistlethwaite makes this assertion with special reference to the early days of our republic, but it is currently applicable in that it illustrates that the state is regarded by Americans as the creation of the people, while in many European countries it is considered to be an independent entity.

From a more critical viewpoint, Jose Ortega y Gasset remarks that in America, unlike Europe, the masses have not felt inferior to a privileged minority, while Guglielmo Ferrero charges that American civilization sacrifices the middle class to the "popular class." A more correct analysis, however, might be that the masses have attained middle class status here as the result of the application of the principles of democracy and the technique of mass production. Of greater validity is the observation of Amaury de Riencourt that in America "one can find an extreme tension between a ruthless materialism and an ethereal idealism," while in Europe "one finds an intermediary stage between materialism and spiritualism, tinged with mild skepticism." Here again one encounters an expression of the belief that Europe stands for moderation and the United States for extremism, and it must be admitted that Americans rarely regard this country as a "golden mean."

Quite a few critics also assert that the European approach to life is more complex than the American. Thus Andre Siegfried points out that Europe "is an ancient and old-fashioned structure, as complicated as an age-old forest encumbered with liana, parasites, and impenetrable brushwood," while "the American background . . . makes one think of the clear, geometrical design of an immense California orchard, all in one block."[68] Americans, of course, often stress their straightforwardness, and they similarly regard European "deviousness" with suspicion. On the other hand, M. J. Bonn maintains that America differs from Europe in that it is optimistic while the latter is skeptical, creative while Europe is preservative, and artificial while the Old World is spontaneous. One might question Bonn's judgment, but couplings of this type are often quite perceptive, despite their occasional inaccuracies.

It must be admitted that the sense of contrast between America and Europe is abetted by certain misconceptions which each has of the other. Thus Alfred Zimmern suggests that "in the Old World it is the habit of regarding America as a vast and semi-barbarous extension of Europe," and "in America the bad tradition takes the form of regarding Europe as a decadent continent." Lucien Romier similarly states that Europeans fail to grasp the real essence of the United States, while M. J. Bonn observes that Americans are too detached from Europe to really understand the latter. It is quite likely that both sides have contributed to the creation of this atmosphere of misundersanding. Thus Odette Keun observes that "we (Europeans) triumphantly put over on America, during an unconscionable time, a preposterous supervaluation of our own culture," while "the Americans, in their turn, thoroughly persuaded us that their material achievements . . . were centuries ahead of ours." Consequently, both sides have abetted a distorted view of the true relationship which exists between the Old World and the New by over-emphasizing their respective merits through propaganda.

Indeed, there are all sorts of conscious and unconscious prejudices which contribute to tensions between the Old World and the New, and an examination of some of these is quite illuminating. In regard to the attitude of Europe towards the United States, Europeans admit that they do not like to be pitied by Americans; resent being told what to do by the inhabitants of this country; are embittered by American immunity to risks; are upset by the thought of being servile to this nation; and in the case of the aristocracy, fear that American democracy will undermine the European social structure. As for the other side, European writers often claim that Americans are suspicious of European sophistication; are contemptuous of Europe because it is not as prosperous as this country; feel that the Old World is incapable of saving itself and thus unworthy of respect; and are of the opinion that Europeans are not trustworthy, since many of the founders of this nation were expelled from the Old World. In addition, Alfred Zimmern observes that relations between America and Europe have never been on an equal basis, and he adds that "inequality begets embarrassment; and true friendship cannot grow up in an atmosphere of embarrasment." Although Rom Landau does suggest that Americans are willing to accept friendly, constructive criticisms from Europeans, he obviously reflects a minority viewpoint, as it is generally admitted abroad that such criticisms usually result in ill will here. But Europeans generally receive American criticisms of them with displeasure—although they usually are reluctant to admit that this is true.

In summation, then, the majority of European analysts obviously feel that the Old World and the New are dissimilar rather than similar. The misconceptions and prejudices noted above support this view, as they reflect numerous intellectual and psychological variations between Americans and Europeans. Moreover, many European thinkers maintain that the differences between the two are increasing rather than diminishing, and if this trend continues, it will become more and more difficult for future historians to treat the United States and Europe as branches of the same civilization. It is also evident that as the distance between Europe and America widens, critics abroad will gain a certain degree of detachment which should provide the basis for more objective evaluations of the United States. On the other hand, dissimilarities often breed hatred, so that this improvement in perspective may be offset by various subjective prejudices. Yet the probability is that European thought on America will continue to be an amalgam of praise and criticism, as there will doubtless be Bruckbergers as well as Duhamels expressing their views on the United States in the years to come.

Chapter XV

AMERICA IN DOUBLE PERSPECTIVE

It is appropriate at this point to compare the ideas Europeans have about the United States with those that Americans hold. Such an approach furnishes an extra point of reference from which to evaluate the theories of contemporary European thinkers about America. Moreover, this technique complements the objective analysis which constitutes the main body of this work and brings the subjective element sharply into focus. It is, in short, rather appropriate that this book should conclude on such a note: what people believe to be true is often as important as what is really true. This is certainly the case with the ideas about the United States which both Americans and Europeans hold.

In regard to the physical setting, it is quite significant that many European thinkers place an almost exaggerated amount of emphasis on natural resources as a factor in the development of American civilization. Americans prefer to believe that they are superior in various ways to Europeans as individuals, but most Europeans apparently feel that whatever degree of ascendancy the United States has achieved is the result of an abundance of physical riches rather than of an excess of human ingenuity. In addition, European commentators often claim that Europe represents time and America space, and they frequently write of the role of the spatial element in American life with what amounts to contempt. This, perhaps, is only logical. Tradition is founded on the element of time, and one of the few areas in which Europe has an advantage over the United States is that it is blessed with a more extensive past. (Or is this a curse?) On the other hand, European critics often conform to the same stereotyped division of America into sections that so characterizes American thinking, and many have apparently been influenced by the ideas of Frederick Jackson Turner. One would surmise that European observers might be a bit more original in their sectional structuring of this nation, as they view this country from a somewhat detached perspective, but such seemingly is not the case.

As for immigration, most Americans still regard the United States as the "Melting Pot of the World," while the European reaction is sharply divided, as many European critics question the assumption that assimilation has actually taken place here. There are, moreover, quite a few European thinkers who insist that racial integration must be an either-or process, but most Americans do not accept this point of view. In contrast, American and European commentators usually agree that there is a Negro problem in the United States, although they approach this situation differently. Americans often complain that since there are few Negroes in Europe proper, Europeans are free to attack the way that Negoes are treated here without fear of counter-criticism. They also charge that many minority groups (such as the Jews) have been persecuted in Europe far more than Negroes have in this country. Europeans probably emphasize this problem to such an extent because they are at times irritated by the exorbitant claims which Americans make in regard to the functioning of democracy here, and they frequently maintain that the treatment of the Negro is a symbol of American imperfection.

As has been noted before, it is difficult to present a comparative examination of the American and European views on the American national character. A few generalizations, however, might be cautiously offered. As for Europeans, many of them apparently regard this country as immature (or youthful) and unbalanced (or one-sided), and their observations have a slightly critical flavor at times. In contrast, most Americans would consider their youthfulness to be proof of a vitality which Europe lacks, while their "one-sidedness" is evidence to them that this nation is free from many of the evils that permeate European life. Furthermore, one obtains the impression that Europeans often regard the American national character as more simple and less paradoxical than its European counterpart. Americans would probably agree with this judgment, as they like to believe themselves as being straightforward and free from deception. One might suggest that while further examination of this subject would doubtless be edifying, Americans will continue to overemphasize the positive and Europeans the negative features of American life.

In regard to American politics, the extent to which American and European commentators are in agreement leads one to conclude that in this particular instance Europeans follow the lead established by Americans instead of striking off on new paths of their own. For example, most Americans probably would concur in the European judgment that political parties in the United States are essentially administrative rather than ideological, although they see nothing wrong with this. Many Americans, moreover, would not question the widespread European charge that politicians here are corrupt, that men of ability refuse to enter politics, and that interest in political activity is intermittent. But apparently most European critics fail to recognize (or tend to ignore) the fact that Americans expect politics to be a slice of life, encompassing both its merits and its faults, rather than an abstract ideological crusade. As far as democracy is concerned, the American image seems to be more sharply defined than the European, probably for the reason that in the past Europeans have been as much absorbed with the problem of overthrowing totalitarian regimes as in formulating abstract ideals. Although Americans may be a bit vague at times as to what they mean when they speak of democracy, Europeans are often even less clear. In fact, democracy to an European may mean anything from constitutional republicanism to pure communism, so that it sometimes appears in the writings of Europeans as more of a cliche than as a definite concept.

American government is another area in which European commentators often have patterned their thinking along American lines. This, however, is to be expected, since politics and government are inextricably interrelated. European observers often refer to the mystic awe with which Americans regard their Constitution, but they obviously have been infected with some of this awe themselves. Moreover, they frequently admit that America's constitutional stability has been much greater than has Europe's. It appears at times, however, that European critics tend to exaggerate the tripartite features of the American national government, while American commentators probably place greater emphasis on the smooth functioning of the three branches as a whole. In addition, European observers are often puzzled by the operation of the federalist system in the United States, but many Americans do not fully understand federalism either. It must, of course, be admitted that the obscurantist character of recent Supreme Court decisions has not helped to clarify matters. Finally, most American writers agree with the basically negative evaluation which their European brethren have made of state and local government in this country, but they still claim that the variety of government found in America is superior to the European brand.

A rather unpleasant exchange of views at times takes place between observers in the Old World and the New in regard to economic activity here. On the one hand, European commentators often charge that Americans sacrifice quality for quantity, and that the material opulence of this nation may be a token of materialism rather than of spirituality. On the other hand, American analysts frequently chide

Europeans for their "sour grapes" attitude, as they maintain that the natural and man-made wealth of this country provides a much stronger foundation for an economic democracy than Europe is able to offer. Of course, a larger proportion of American than European thinkers are pro-capitalist; this fact accounts for some of the divergence of opinion over the economic system in operation in the United States. Yet, to be perfectly fair, it must be admitted that Americans are aware that their economic blessings may lead to spiritual bankruptcy, but many of them also believe that material and spiritual wealth may exist side by side. For this reason Americans sometimes become incensed when Europeans claim that the Old World is spiritually richer although materially poorer than the New, as a failure to produce outwardly may be a sign of inner poverty.

The subject of radicalism also has provoked considerable disagreement among American and European observers. This lack of consensus, however, should be largely attributed to the different perspectives from which the two sides view this question. American critics are perhaps less impressed by the relative absence of radicalism from this nation than are their European counterparts, mainly because Americans exaggerate the significance of the limited radical activity that does take place here. On the other hand, Americans usually agree with the widespread European opinion that the Old World and the New are essentially different, but they bitterly resent the attempt of various European commentators to pair the United States with the Soviet Union. It is admittedly true that Americans are rather touchy on the subjects of radicalism and Russia, but continental "McCarthyphobia," suggests that Europeans do not always treat these topics with what can be considered cold objectivity. On the other hand, it is probably true that radicalism and Russia do not carry as strong a connotation of "taboo" among Europeans as they do among Americans; consequently Europeans are able to discuss both subjects a bit more dispassionately.

The New Deal is seemingly a puzzle to both domestic and foreign analysts. There apparently is little consensus either here or abroad as to whether the Rooseveltian reforms were original or imitative, conservative or radical, experimental or doctrinaire. One might surmise that European erities would tend to play down the significance of the New Deal. This is for the reason that the European historical tradition has been so permeated with radicalism in recent years that the Rooseveltian reforms would appear to be of a relatively mild character when viewed from this perspective. Likewise, the fact that radical experimentation has been the exception rather than the rule in American life might lead one to predict that American critics would be prone to exaggerate the radical features of the New Deal. Yet a cross-section of European thought on the Rooseveltian reforms bears a striking resemblance to a cross-section of American thought, and thus preconceived theories as to how Europeans and Americans should react to the New Deal are invalidated by the facts. It is also significant that the passage of a quarter of a century has accomplished little other than to take the edge off some of the more extreme European observations on the Rooseveltian reforms. Moreover, there apparently is no more chance of European critics coming to a consensus in the near future on the New Deal than there is of their American counterparts reaching an agreement.

Turning now to the field of foreign policy, Europeans, like Americans, generally divide United States global relations into imperialist, isolationist, and internationalist phases, but their interpretations of these phases differ from the standard American analyses. Thus Americans as a rule do not deny that there has been an imperialist element in American foreign policy, but they usually claim that its influence has generally been limited to the political sphere. On the other hand, Europeans often maintain that this nation has exerted itself in an economically and ideologically imperialist manner as well. As for isolationism, American commentators usually cover its entire history, while their European counterparts generally emphasize the period between 1919 and 1941. Of course, European observations on these two phases of American global policy are rarely received here with indifference, since many Americans regard criticisms of American imperialism as hypocritical. In addition, they consider attacks on American isolationism to be tokens of a selfish disappointment that this nation did not clean up the mess which Europeans themselves made.

As far as internationalism is concerned, most Europeans feel that it is the duty of the United States to commit itself globally, but they resent too intense an American interest in European affairs. This latter point is borne out by the hostile European reaction to many aspects of the Wilsonian program of international reform, as well as by the displeasure with which Europeans often receive American criticisms of European colonial policy. On the other hand, Americans apparently feel that when they become involved internationally they should go all out, and they often regard European charges of tactlessness as manifestations of a morbid sensitiveness. This is another example of the American tendency to behave in an extreme manner, while Europeans usually act with moderation. Moreover, Americans correlate their assumption of global responsibility with membership in an international organization to promote peace more than Europeans do, since the latter had been playing the game of world politics for centuries before the establishment of such a body.

The topic of religion has perhaps provoked the most violent controversy among American and European commentators, as the widespread American sentiment that this nation is essentially religious is frequently challenged abroad. Here the emphasis that Europeans place on quality is particularly in evidence. Europeans claim (and rightly so) that in the realm of the spirit mere appearances do not count, and many Americans are often seized by an awareness that their vaunted religiosity may be an empty facade. It might be suggested, however, that Americans regard religion as an element that should permeate life as a whole, especially in the field of morals and ethics, while Europeans often compartmentalize religion to the point where its influence is limited to the ecclesiastical realm. On the other hand, American analysts frequently charge that the growing ascendancy of skepticism in the Old World has rendered European thinkers defensive in regard to religious matters. Thus it is not surprising that their observations are biased and distorted at times.

Both American and European critics seemingly overemphasize the originality of the more recent American philosophical tradition, although they differ in their estimates of its beneficial influence. Most Americans like to believe themselves to be idealists, but Europeans often claim that at times we are idealistic to the extent that effective action is rendered impossible. In addition, European commentators detect more of a contradiction than do Americans in the presence of both idealistic and pragmatic elements in American life. This is partly for the reason that what may appear to be an inconsistency in theory may not be so in practice. Some of the material presented in the twelfth chapter, moreover, reveals that Europeans appear to be somewhat confused at times as to the exact meaning of pragmatism, instrumentalism, and utilitarianism, while Americans deal with these philosophical concepts in a more facile manner. Of course, Europeans do not regard this nation to be as materialist as Americans think that they do, but most of them still place a greater emphasis on American materialism than do Americans. The latter, however, generally believe that this stress is proof either than Europeans are envious or that they are ignorant that material riches may be a form of spiritual blessing.

As for intellectual life, Europeans usually regard education and culture as subdivisions of a larger whole, while Americans tend more to treat the two as separate entities. Admittedly Americans show concern at times that the classical element in education is being neglected here, but they have few doubts that they surpass European education from the utilitarian point of view. On the other hand, Europeans tend to emphasize that a utilitarian education is only a second-rate education, if it is an education at all, while they usually consider the classical tradition in America as deficient. In regard to culture, most American and European commentators admit that the American cultural tradition was once highly imitative, but a large number of them recognize that it is now becoming more original. American analysts, however, stress the latter point more than European critics do. As for intellectual life in general, it has been pointed out that Europeans still think that they have an edge on the Americans in the realm of the mind, but many Americans probably feel that Europeans devote too much time to barren theorizing.

Referring back to the previous chapter, it should be added that many Americans believe that the apparently increasing schism between the Old World and the New is a blessing, as this nation has been attempting to assert its spiritual independence from Europe for two centuries. It is a bit more difficult to determine how Europeans react to this widening gap, but they probably view this process with resentment, since the movement of the United States towards autonomy has been accompanied by a decrease in European prestige. The fact that the writings chosen for inclusion in this volume are all of post-World War I vintage is not coincidental, as this great conflict finally confirmed the growing realization both here and abroad that America was edging further and further away from Europe. Of course, since that date there have been increased diplomatic, economic, and intellectual contacts between the Old World and the New, and few critics either here or abroad would deny this, but a step-up in contacts is no guarantee of a growing spiritual togetherness.

It is hoped that these observations on the American image as viewed from both sides of the Atlantic reveal how large a role the element of perspective plays in the evaluation of any historical situation. What is so noteworthy, however, is not that Europeans and Americans differ in their judgments on various features of American life, but that they at times do agree—and agree much more frequently than one might imagine. It is highly significant that thinkers here concur in many European criticisms of this nation, as this demonstrates that Americans are aware of their faults as well as their virtues. Admittedly this agreement is often the result of European thinkers copying American ideas, and this process is not always desirable, since these ideas are not always accurate. But Americans and Europeans at times do reach similar conclusions on American life independently. Although it may seem a bit paradoxical, it is quite conceivable that a closer degree of understanding may develop between the Old World and the New as they move away from each other. This term, of course, is used here to denote intellectual comprehension rather than emotional rapport.

Certain obstacles stand in the way of a closer degree of understanding, however, particularly the imperfect manner in which the ideas of European thinkers on America are disseminated here. In the first place, American commentators often pay too little attention to those European tomes which do not deal with the politics or government of the United States, although many important works have been written outside these two fields. Secondly, American critics frequently concentrate on showy but superficial studies of American life penned by Europeans (take your choice), while such profound volumes as Hermann von Keyserling's *America Set Free* gather dust on the library shelves. Thirdly, a disturbing number of American writers restrict themselves to such nineteenth century observers as Bryce and de Tocqueville when they refer to European thought on the United States, despite the fact that many trans-Atlantic authorities on American life have come into prominence in recent years. As a result, Americans are often left uninformed or misinformed as to what modern European thinkers have to say about this country. Moreover, they sometimes compensate for this deficiency by making faulty conjectures of their own as to what particular image of the United States is currently in vogue abroad. The misunderstanding which exists between the Old World and the New, therefore, might be blamed as much on the distorted manner in which Americans interpret European observations as on what Americans actually write.

In closing, the author would like to single out as especially outstanding several of the more recent European commentators on America. He hesitates at doing this, mainly because it is a quite hazardous process to make such a selection, but he nevertheless feels that such an appraisal is necessary. As far as sheer originality is concerned, Arnold Toynbee and Hermann von Keyserling perhaps should be rated first, although their more imaginative theories are not always valid. In addition, the studies of Hilaire Belloc and Wyndham Lewis are quite original. As for comprehensiveness, Denis Brogan and

Harold Laski unquestionably head the list, although Andre Siegfried does not rank far behind. But all three authors, despite the near universality of their coverage, have their special fields of interest, as Laski and Brogan concentrate on politics and government, Siegfried on economics and immigration. Significantly, originality and comprehensiveness are not always found together in the writings of European analysts of the United States, and this is the reason why a two-fold system of classification is used here.

Other European commentators, however, have also produced works on this nation which are quite worthy additions to the literature. One might cite here the studies of M. J. Bonn, Raymond Bruckberger, Bernard Fay, Geoffrey Gorer, Jacques Maritain, and Lucien Romier. Of course, any given author's *corpus* of writings is not always of uniform quality, and an examination of the outputs of Andre Maurois and Frank Thistlethwaite demonstrate that European students of American life often produce mediocre results when they attempt to write standard histories. But even a few of the "anti-American" critics have penned works which are "classics," such as George Duhamel's *America the Menace* and Lucien Lehman's *The American Illusion*. There are, of course, numerous books and articles of limited value, but these are generally so because they lack fresh insights rather than because they distort the facts. Indeed, one might be surprised at the degree to which the overwhelming majority of the writings of European observers on the United States are factually accurate, although the analyses contained in them are often far from valid. But on the other hand, European studies of American life are only incidentally depositories of fact; they are primarily interpretations.

Modern European thought on the United States, therefore, is a mixture of the brilliant and the undistinguished, the perceptive and the distorted, the colorful and the dull. As it is unfair to judge it by its lowest common denominator, it is also unjust to rate it by its occasional flashes of genius. If one were to evaluate it as a whole, he might suggest that European critics have pictured America more competently than one might expect, but that there is still considerable room for improvement. A similar study of recent American thought on Europe, however, would probably reveal that our evaluations of European life possess similar virtues and shortcomings. It is unreasonable, therefore, to expect that European commentators would produce flawless portrayals of the United States. In any event, an examination of their appraisals adds to our knowledge of America. Many an important point has been missed by native-born writers who choose to disregard what others have to say about us.

CHAPTER XVI

THE QUESTION OF PRESTIGE

Apart from the subjects discussed in the text, there are at least three other topics which merit separate treatment here. In the first place, the prestige polls which were such a controversial issue in the 1960 Presidential race require special analysis, as many misconceptions exist in regard to them. Secondly, the relationship between present day and past criticisms of the United States needs to be clarified further, since most Americans are unaware that many of these diverse judgments are not new. Finally, the effect of the dynamics of global change on American prestige should be examined at greater length, for analysts all too frequently interpret our international standing in terms of a popularity contest between the Russians and ourselves. All of these points are touched on throughout the text, but this in no way lessens the desirability of a more elaborate discussion of them.

It is only appropriate that the prestige polls be dealt with first, since the acrimonious dispute which they generated a year or so ago was the factor which first made us conscious and concerned about what foreigners think of us. The fact that President Eisenhower suppressed them during his tenure as chief executive doubtless helped to insure their immortality, but this action also created an atmosphere of mystery and intrigue in which it was impossible to analyze them dispassionately and objectively. It is thus not surprising that commentators tend either to ignore them or to overestimate their significance. The truth is, of course, that these documents are an important manifestation of the dimming of the American image abroad, but they are only a symptom, not the cause of this loss in stature. For this reason, they serve as a valuable starting point in any examination of the question of prestige, although they should not be regarded as the last word on the topic.

Inasmuch as most critics have not actually read the original United States Information Agency documents of June and October 10, 1960, it is appropriate to present an extended analysis of the two reports which first catapulted the prestige polls into the headlines. These documents differ somewhat; the first is rather general as to subject matter and confined to samplings from western Europe, while the second concentrates on the satellite race although it purportedly mirrors global attitudes. In addition, the relatively long initial study places an emphasis on statistics which the second does not. For these and other reasons, it is wise to discuss the two separately, despite the fact that they are interrelated to a considerable extent.

The first USIA report (June 1960) is evidently based on 2150 interviews conducted in Great Britain and France late in May of that year. Moreover, it is concerned mostly with contemporary events such as the collapse of the summit meeting and the U-2 incident rather than with more fundamental considerations. Analysts both here and abroad have, of course, pointed out that this document signals a loss in American prestige, but many of them have failed to note that it also stresses that Russia's international standing has suffered a corresponding decline which may be more serious than ours. The fact that half of those who were interviewed failed to express a preference for either the United States or the Soviet Union is perhaps even more noteworthy; it demonstrates that European neutralism is a highly potent force today. Such neutralism may have been stimulated by a growing fear abroad of war.

In addition, the first USIA report reveals that there is an increasing dubiousness in Great Britain and France as to our capacity to exert global leadership, mainly for the reason that it is recognized there that our military strength is being challenged by the Soviet Union. Even more surprising, however, is the fact that interviewees in these two countries frequently question the veracity of the United States, although not as often as they challenge that of Russia. That such a sentiment is widespread is quite naturally upsetting to Americans, for we like to believe that we represent ourselves abroad in a truthful manner. European skepticism as to our capacities, however, is not reflected in a softening attitude towards communism, since the British and the French have held firm in their adherence to NATO, and have become even more tolerant of American troops being stationed abroad. These highly striking findings might best be explained on the grounds that Europeans feel that their defenses should be strengthened so as to offset various American weaknesses.

The second USIA report (October 10, 1960), which purportedly reflects world opinion as a whole, is based on several subsidiary studies rather than upon original compilation. No indication, however, is given as to the number of interviewees polled. This document, which is focused on the satellite race, emphasizes that there is a widespread sentiment in most parts of the free world that the Soviet Union leads the United States in spatial achievements and is threatening our overall scientific and technological supremacy. Aside from the question of space, the second USIA report also suggests that many individuals overseas feel that the U. S. S. R. has narrowed the economic gap between itself and America. Such a claim, of course, is anathema to us. It is also noteworthy that this study theorizes that a belief exists globally that the Russians have a greater faith in communism than we have in democracy, and that they work harder to effect their ends than we do. Americans doubtless are less prone to challenge this finding than they are certain others, since there has been considerable grumbling here that we have failed to dedicate ourselves as a nation to the extent that we should have.

Admittedly the material presented in these reports is not reassuring to us, but when it is placed in the proper perspective it loses some of its alarmist character. In the first place, neither USIA report represents a blanket condemnation of the United States, but deals only with American shortcomings in specific areas. The fact that data favorable to this nation is almost totally excluded from both documents, moreover, provides grounds for suspicion as to their objectivity, since it indicates that they were drawn up to support a previously arrived at hypothesis rather than to present all sides of the question of prestige. Another important consideration which must be reckoned with is that each release is focused on our competitive struggle with the Soviet Union, although this is not the only factor which affects our international standing. Finally, these reports give the impression that most of the overseas criticisms of the United States are of recent vintage, when in fact many of them date back to an era in which our image abroad was more lustrous.

The significance of this point is so great that it must be elaborated on at length. If many of the current adverse judgments directed against this country overseas are not new, this would indicate that there are factors involved in our recent loss of prestige other than our shortcomings. The author, moreover, is firmly convinced that the decline in stature which we are experiencing today is not solely attributable to our faults, and he will devote the final third of the postscript to developing this theory at some length. First of all, however, it is necessary to prove that foreign criticisms of America are to a large extent rooted in the past, although they are currently set in a different context than they were a decade or a generation ago. While it would be possible to deal with adverse judgments in numerous fields, it was decided that the essential point would be made by references to the social, scientific, economic, and diplomatic areas.

In regard to integration, the failure of the Negro to obtain an educational status equal to that of the white man has long been regarded abroad as proof that democratic ideals and social realities do not always coincide in the United States. Thus adverse judgments in this sector are not new. In recent years, of course, the Negro has begun to demand equality in an increasing number of other areas, and this has intensified overseas criticisms of the way that the racial problem is handled here. But the factor which has really thrown this issue into sharp focus has been the recent growth of "black democracies" in Africa. Since they have been alienated by the way that their brethren are "mistreated" here by the white man, the colored people of the Dark Continent are perpetually tempted to reject the American variety of democracy for the Soviet brand. This possibility is particularly distasteful to anti-communist Europeans, who accuse us of goading Africa into the arms of the communists through our racial policies, and it must be admitted that their condemnation is not unwarranted.

As for science, Europeans have always been somewhat suspicious of the scientific achievements of this country, since it generally has been Europeans (Einstein, Fermi, etc.) rather than Americans who have made the truly original contributions. This attitude, moreover, has not been dispelled by the work of the Oppenheimers and the Salks, whose efforts have raised America to the very zenith of the scientific firmament. Foreign doubts as to our abilities thus existed in the field of science prior to the fall of 1957, when they were crystallized by the lauching of the first Soviet space satellite. Admittedly Russian successes in the exploration of the aerial sea do not constitute a wholesale denial of American achievements in the scientific sector, but they are naturally interpreted globally as evidence that our claims to undisputed leadership are somewhat inflated.

Economically the situation is a bit more complex. It is true that America has experienced recessions and even depressions in the past, but we eventually recovered from them even though we suffered a temporary loss in economic prestige. The dollar has declined in value before (as when F. D. R. reduced its gold content), and Europeans have become upset more than once when American sentiment shifted in the direction of protection (as is evidenced by their protests against our numerous high tariffs). In recent years, however, we have experienced economic difficulties while Europe has been enjoying material prosperity; this consideration has had a profound effect on criticisms directed against us from abroad.

As far as diplomacy is concerned, the crucial issue is not that the forces of democracy under the leadership of the United States have begun to lose ground to the communists, because this has been happening intermittently since 1945. Eastern Europe, continental China, North Korea, Tibet, and a part of what was once French Indo-China all have fallen to the Marxists, but as none of this territory is located within the Western Hemisphere (and thus under our jurisdiction), foreign observers have not assigned the responsibility for these losses entirely to us. The emergence of the Castro regime in Cuba, on the other hand, places matters in an entirely different light, as for the first time since 1823 our ascendancy in this hemisphere is being seriously threatened. Admittedly the control of such a small island may seem of little consequence when viewed from a global perspective, but it has been by the means of such a small opening as this that the communists have scored significant successes in the past, and overseas analysts apparently do not discount the possibility of this catastrophe being reenacted in our own backyard.

In all of the above examples, it is noteworthy that it has been the successes of some other nation or nations even more so than failures on our own part which were responsible for world opinion becoming more sharply focused on our shortcomings. This is a highly significant point, but it is far too often overlooked by those alarmists who place the blame for the decline which we have suffered in prestige solely on our shoulders. The external challenge, moreover, comes from a different source in each case, since Africa, Russia, Europe and Cuba provide the threat to us in the social, scientific, economic, and diplomatic sectors respectively. It is noteworthy that in only one of the four instances accomplishments on the part of the Soviet Union itself are responsible for the tarnishing of our image, although one might justifiably regard Cuba as a Soviet appendage. Thus having disposed of the fallacy that foreign criticisms of this nation represent newly arrived at adverse judgments, we may now lay to rest the myth that it is Russia alone which presents a challenge to our prestige.

It was pointed out in the introduction that the author believes that the years between 1919 and 1960 constitute a new completed historical epoch. He thinks, moreover, that the real significance of the prestige polls of 1960 is that they represent a global acknowledgement that the almost unchallenged ascendancy which we have enjoyed since the close of World War I is now at an end. The material which has just been presented provides evidence in support of this hypothesis. This in no way implies that we are on the verge of entering the ranks of the second rate nations, as in all probability the United States will continue to maintain its status as a Great Power. It must be recognized, however, that developments which are taking place and will continue to take place elsewhere will divert a certain amount of global leadership away from America, and this is bound to have an effect on our prestige abroad.

Moreover, indications are that mankind is on the threshold of a new epoch in which progress will not be confined mainly to the United States and Western Europe, as it has been in the past, but will become more world-wide in scope. Evidence in support of this prophecy is so substantial as to be almost incontrovertible. As a result, the countries of the globe in the years to come will not regard America as the embodiment of a more advanced way of life to the degree that they once did, for they themselves will personify this more and more. Quite a few of us may find this probability discomforting, since it will be accompanied by an alteration of our image abroad. Such a development, however, does not constitute a Kiplingian *Recessional* for the stereotype of America as the symbol of progress, but what future respect we will be able to command will stem from the fact that we provided the testing ground on which a more advanced way of life was first brought to fruition, not that we will eternally monopolize it.

Yet though it may be necessary for us to adjust to the global realities of the second half of the twentieth century, there is no reason for Americans to be pessimists, since the existence of a few obstacles does not preclude the possibility of an optimistic outlook. It is quite likely, for example, that most, if not all, of our current problems will be solved in the next decade or so. Thus advances will be made in the race into space, the Negro will better himself socially and economically, there will be an upswing in the economic cycle, and a new non-communist government may seize power in Cuba. But as has just been pointed out, our future achievements, in contrast to those of the past, will not be judged globally against a backdrop of a relative lack of performance on the part of other countries. For this reason, we must assert ourselves to an even greater extent than ever before if we wish to gain the plaudits of the remainder of the world, since it will be only through a dynamic program of continual growth that we will be able to offer proof positive of our greatness.

REFERENCES

1. J. A. Spender likewise writes of the lack of permanence in the life of this nation.

2. Geoffrey Gorer, M. J. Bonn, and Philip Gibbs are trans-Atlantic writers who emphasize the differences between the various sections of America.

3. Denis Brogan, on the other hand, suggests that a correlation should be drawn between a high tariff and limited immigration, although his reasoning is a bit faulty.

4. Denis Brogan also maintains that the United States no longer embodies the hopes of the masses abroad.

5. Oswald Spengler might be cited as another anti-assimilationist.

6. Russell, of course, personally experienced some of this discrimination during his trips to this country.

7. Alfred Zimmern is another European commentator whose ideas parallel those of von Keyserling in this particular case.

8. Denis Brogan links persecution of dissent with social integration, an American characteristic which Belloc commented on earlier in this chapter.

9. Fay is decidedly in the minority in this matter.

10. Georges Duhamel claims that the American has not suffered enough to be great.

11. Von Keyserling theorizes that Americans are tending towards a "termatoid state."

12. Harold Laski is of the same belief.

13. On the other hand, Denis Brogan opines that Americans have explained themselves to the world from the first, but many critics would question that they have been truly successful in their attempt.

14. Von Keyserling makes the rather curious observation that Americans must above all become reverent.

15. But Geoffrey Gorer claims that individuals here are expected to go into politics for their own personal advantage.

16. Brogan considers the Byrd "machine" of Virginia to be the most perfectly functioning state machine in this country, a view betraying his leftist orientation.

17. Here Chesterton draws a parallel between the American Constitution and the Spanish Inquisition.

18. Hilaire Belloc considers this to be the most egalitarian nation in the world.

19. Arnold Toynbee also advocates this hypothesis.

20. H. A. L. Fisher, on the other hand, writes of a diminishing reverence for the Constitution here.

21. This, of course, is a typically leftist sentiment.

22. Harold Laski maintains that most strong Presidents result from political protests, a quite justified claim.

23. Laski feels that the United States is apparently unable to convert from individualism to statism.

24. For an affirmation of the existence of the right of freedom of discussion here, consult H. G. Wells.

25. Lewis Namier is another critic who stresses the key role of the economic element here.

26. Bernard Fay regards Henry Ford as the prophet of a new religion.

27. Concerning this point Lucien Romier writes that goods must be better as well as cheaper.

28. Hilaire Belloc makes the curious claim that Americans resent Big Business more than Europeans do.

29. M. J. Bonn links this decline to the corresponding drop in immigrants, although this correlation is questionable.

30. Harold Laski, moreover, is not optimistic about future American economic attitudes.

31. It must be admitted that this relationship has changed somewhat recently.

32. For a similar point of view, consult Denis Brogan.

33. Ernest Teilhac, for instance.

34. Salvador de Madariaga is of a diametrically opposite opinion.

35. Halvdan Koht expresses the hope that American "individualism" and Russian "collectivism" will be united in the years to come.

36. Hermann von Keyserling claims that Russia is America's historical ally.

37. Cole notes elsewhere that both the United States and the Soviet Union lack internal economic barriers.

38. Denis Brogan also maintains that the New Deal was experimental rather than doctrinaire.

39. But as Arnold Toynbee writes, European nations made no protest against this expansion.

40. Barbara Ward also makes this significant point.

41. Philip Gibbs likewise stresses this fact.

42. Hilaire Belloc, John Maynard Keynes, and Gunnar Myrdal are of a similar opinion.

43. Max Beloff refers to the presence here in the post-World War II period of a feeling that the United States is a "beleagured garrison"—an attitude highly characteristic of isolationists.

44. Laski partly atones for this error two pages later.

45. Bernard Fay also makes this point.

46. This point is similarly emphasized by Raoul de Roussy de Sales. Amaury de Riencourt, on the other hand, stresses Franklin Roosevelt's isolationist tendencies.

47. Harold Laski maintains that World War II solved the unemployment problem in America.

48. Laski makes the characteristic claim that American business men are wary of international atomic controls.

49. Denis de Rougemont predicts that the eventual end of the Cold War will be followed by an alignment of the United States and the Soviet Union against China.

50. Laski here refers to Reinhold Niebuhr.

51. Luigi Barzini feels that Americans underestimate the difficulty involved in overcoming evil.

52. One might note here Bernard Fay's curious remark that American agnostics prefer the Catholics to the Protestants.

53. Perhaps Laski and Bonn exaggerate matters.

54. Frank Thistlethwaite is of a similar opinion.

55. This in no way invalidates the claim of G. K. Chesterton that Americans have a love for measurement.

56. Frank Thistlethwaite likewise stresses this not unjustified theory.

57. This may be, as Lucien Romier suggests, because intellectual activity means little to the masses.

58. Denis Brogan maintains that our schools teach "living" rather than knowledge.

59. G. K. Chesterton believes that Englishmen know more about American literature than American history.

60. As is pointed out by Bertrand Russell.

61. This factor is emphasized by Arnold Toynbee.

62. As is stressed by Rom Landau.

63. Lucien Romier makes the rather curious claim that France and America are the only two successful democratic republics.

64. Check in this connection the opening of the sixth chapter.

65. Koht also refers to the Belgian Constitution of 1830.

66. Richard Muller-Freienfels similarly emphasizes American influence in the social area.

67. Jose Ortega y Gasset is another European analyst who is of this opinion.

68. Harold Laski also raises this point of simplicity versus complexity.

BIBLIOGRAPHY

BOOKS

Angell, Norman, *The Steep Places* (London: Hamish Hamilton, 1947), 207 pp. An examination of the post-war world with an emphasis on the sometimes antagonistic relations between the United States and Great Britain.

Angell, Norman, *Let The People Know* (New York: The Viking Press, 1943), 245 pp. One of the many books inspired by the outbreak of World War II.

Angell, Norman, and others, *The United States and Great Britain* (Chicago: University of Chicago Press, 1932), 235 pp. The third in a series of works on American foreign policy published by the Chicago Council on Foreign Relations.

Aron, Raymond, and August Hecksher, *Diversity of Worlds* (New York: Reynal and Company, 1957), 176 pp. This volume grew out of a conference held at Arden House, New York, in 1956 which was attended by various French and American scholars and leaders of opinion.

Aron, Raymond, *On War* (New York: Doubleday and Company, 1959), 143 pp. Appearing in the Anchor Books series, this monograph is one of the outstanding analyses of current military and diplomatic tensions. Translated by Terence Kilmartin.

Aron, Raymond, *The Opium of the Intellectuals* (London: Secker and Warburg, 1957) 324 pp. Aron here lays bare the shortcomings and follies of the intelligentsia. Translated by Terence Kilmartin.

Barraclough, Geoffrey, *History in a Changing World* (Norman: University of Oklahoma Press, 1956), 246 pp. A quasi-Spenglerian examination of modern history in which the idea of progress and scientific history serve as two of the focal points of attack.

Barzini, Luigi, *Americans Are Alone in the World* (New York: Random House, 1953), 209 pp. A best seller in Italy in its original form, this book has a pro-American bias despite its criticisms of the United States.

Beauvoir, Simone de, *America Day by Day* (New York: Grove Press, 1953), 337 pp. The result of a four months' stay in the United States, de Beauvoir's volume presents this country from what might be labelled as the feminine existentialist viewpoint.

Belloc, Hilaire, *The Contrast* (New York: Robert M. McBride and Company, 1924), 257 pp. Based in part on first-hand experience of this nation, *The Contrast* is one of the outstanding expressions of the thesis that America and Europe are essentially different.

Beloff, Max, *The American Federal Government* (New York: Oxford University Press, 1959), 213 pp. A standard treatment focused on the national level which has the advantage of up-to-date coverage.

Beloff, Max, *Foreign Policy and the Democratic Process* (Baltimore: The Johns Hopkins Press, 1955), 134 pp. Beloff's opus represents the Albert Shaw Lectures on Diplomatic History for 1954, and one of the key ideas set forth here is that there exists a fundamental conflict in America between the democratic process and the implementation of foreign policy.

Bonn, M. J., *The American Adventure* (New York: The John Day Company, 1934),
318 pp. Subtitled "A Study of Bourgeois Civilization," Bonn's book represents one
of the leading efforts of its kind. Translated by Mabel Brailsford.

Bonn, M. J., *Amerika und Sein Problem* (Munchen: Meyer and Jessen, 1925), 176 pp.
This volume is centered around the problem caused by the migration of individuals
with varied backgrounds from Europe to the United States.

Bonn, M. J., *The Crisis of Capitalism in America* (New York: The John Day Company, 1932), 232 pp. A study dealing with the depression of 1929 and its effect
on the future of capitalism in America. Translated by Winifred Ray.

Bonn, M. J., *Whither Europe?* (New York: Philosophical Library, 1952), 207 pp.
Bonn here stresses American anti-colonialism and foreign relations in general.

Brogan, Denis W., *The American Character* (New York: Alfred A. Knopf, 1944), 169
pp. Elucidating but improvisatory, this is one of Brogan's most important studies
of the United States.

Brogan, Denis W., *American Themes* (New York: Harper and Brothers, 1949), 284 pp.
A collection of various newspaper and periodical pieces which first appeared in print
between 1931 and 1947.

Brogan, Denis W., *Citizenship Today* (Chapel Hill: The University of North Carolina
Press, 1960), 116 pp. This volume consists of the Weil Lectures on American
Citizenship of the University of North Carolina for 1959.

Brogan, Denis W., *The Crisis of American Federalism* (Glasgow: Jackson, Son and
Company, 1944), 43 pp. An essay which in its original form was the tenth Lecture
on the David Murray Foundation in the University of Glasgow.

Brogan, Denis W., *The Era of Franklin D. Roosevelt* (New Haven: Yale University
Press, 1950), 382 pp. A good introduction to the New Deal, but rather sketchy
for the period after 1940.

Brogan, Denis W., *The Free State* (New York: Alfred A. Knopf, 1945), 130 pp.
A meditation on the problem of reconstructing post-war Germany, with quite a few
references of significance to the United States.

Brogan, Denis W., *Government of the People* (New York: Harper and Brothers, 1933),
415 pp. Dedicated to Harold Laski, this study was the first extensive work that
Brogan wrote on the American scene.

Brogan, Denis W., *Politics and Law in the United States* (Cambridge: The University
Press, 1941), 127 pp. Brogan here discusses the Constitution, American political
parties, the Presidency and the Congress, and the function of the Supreme Court.

Brogan, Denis W., *Politics in America* (New York: Harper and Brothers, 1954),
407 pp. More optimistic in tone than *Government of the People,* this volume still
covers much of the ground dealt with in the earlier study.

Brogan, Denis W., *The Price of Revolution* (London: Hamish Hamilton, 1951), 280
pp. An analysis of whether or not the consequent ends justify the revolutionary
means, this monograph also has a chapter on post-World War II America.

Brogan, Denis W., *U.S.A.* (London: Oxford University Press, 1941), 144 pp. A
brief but kaleidoscopic examination of the American scene.

Bruckberger, Raymond, *One Sky to Share* (New York: P. J. Kennedy and Sons, 1952)
248 pp. The half of this work devoted to life here is a prefatory sketch of *Image of
America,* although it is worth reading in its own right. Translated by Dorothy Carr
Howell.

Bruckberger, Raymond, *Image of America* (New York: The Viking Press, 1959),
277 pp. Probably one of the most original and perceptive books ever written on

the United States, Bruckberger's volume places great emphasis on the economic factor.

Bryce, James, *Modern Democracies*, 2 volumes (New York: The Macmillan Company, 1921). Bryce places considerable emphasis on American democracy in the major effort of his old age.

Bryce, James, *The Study of American History* (New York: The Macmillan Company, 1922), 118 pp. An extended essay originally delivered as the inaugural lecture of the Sir George Watson Chair of American History, Literature, and Institutions.

Chesterton, G. K., *What I Saw in America* (New York: Dodd, Mead and Company, 1922), 297 pp. This interesting volume consists of a series of loosely related pieces dealing with various aspects of American life.

Cobban, Alfred, *National Self-Determination* (London: Oxford University Press, 1945), 185 pp. Cobban stresses the importance of the American Revolution and the Civil War in the development of the concept of self-determination, and he also examines the role that Wilson played at Versailles.

Cole, G. D. H., *Europe, Russia, and the Future* (New York: The Macmillan Company, 1942), 233 pp. An expression of the hope for a socialist Europe in which the United States plays the role of the capitalist scapegoat.

Cole, G. D. H., *A Guide Through World Chaos* (New York: Alfred A. Knopf, 1932) 554 pp. Another economic study which shows a surprising confidence (in that it was written by a socialist) in the health of the American economy.

Cole, G. D. H., *The Second International, 1889-1914* (London: Macmillan and Company, 1950), Part I 518 pp.; Part II 525 pp. The third installment of Cole's monumental *A History of Socialist Thought*, this definitive work devotes a lengthy chapter to socialism in America during this period.

Cole, G. D. H., *World in Transition* (New York: Oxford University Press, 1949), 646 pp. This book might be described as a post-World War II counterpart of *A Guide Through World Chaos*.

Crossman, R. H. S., *The Charm of Politics* (New York: Harper and Brothers, 1958) 243 pp. An interesting and quite original collection of essays, many of them dealing with key American personalities.

Duhamel, George, *America the Menace* (Boston: Houghton Mifflin Company, 1931), 217 pp. One of the outstanding anti-American books of the post-1918 period. Translated by Charles Miner Thompson.

Fay, Bernard, *Roosevelt and His America* (Boston: Little, Brown, and Company, 1933), 345 pp. Written just after F. D. R. took office, this volume in general praises Roosevelt and lambasts the Republicans.

Ferrero, Guglielmo, *The Unity of the World* (New York; Albert and Charles Boni, 1930) 196 pp. Ferrero here stresses "World Americanization" in a study which analyzes the integration of the globe. Translated by Howard Coxe.

Fisher, H. A. L., *Pages from the Past* (Oxford: The Clarendon Press, 1939), 237 pp. The pertinent essays in this collection are "America after fifteen years" and "Politicians."

Gibbs, Philip, editor, *Bridging the Atlantic* (New York: Doubleday, Doran and Company, 1944), 274 p. This tome consists of a group of sketches contributed by writers from both England and the United States; Gibbs personally penned the second chapter.

Gibbs, Philip, *More That Must Be Told* (New York: Harper and Brothers, 1921),

408 pp.   Still another collection of pieces of limited length, although all were
written by Gibbs himself.
Gibbs, Philip, *People of Destiny* (New York: Harper and Brothers, 1920), 198 pp.
A work of only mediocre quality in which the best chapter is the one entitled
"What England Thinks of America."
Gorer, Geoffrey, *The American People* (New York: W. W. Norton and Company,
1948), 246 pp.   A noted British anthropologist views the United States from the
point of view of cultural anthropology.
Guedalla, Philip, *Conquistador* (New York: Harper and Brothers, 1928), 276 pp.
Subtitled "American Fantasia," this loosely-organized volume is based on a three
months' stay in this country.
Guedalla, Philip, *The Hundredth Year* (New York: Doubleday, Doran and Company,
1939), 312 pp.   An analysis of epochal events (including the re-election of F. D. R.)
which took place during the year 1936.
Jouvenel, Bertrand de, *On Power* (New York: The Viking Press, 1949), 421 pp.
De Jouvenel's monograph attacks the current tendency towards the accumulation
of power in the hands of the central government, and in the process the author
makes quite a few interesting observations on the United States.   Translated by
J. P. Huntington.
Jungk, Robert, *Tomorrow is Already Here* (New York: Simon and Schuster, 1954),
241 pp.   A study of scientific "totalitarianism" in the United States.
Keun, Odette, *A Foreigner Looks at the TVA* (New York: Longmans, Green and
Company, 1937), 89 pp.   The Tennessee Valley Authority as viewed by a noted
European liberal.
Keun, Odette, *I Think Aloud in America* (London: Longmans, Green and Company,
1939), 337 pp.   A later and more extensive elaboration of the ideas set forth in
the prior study.
Keynes, John Maynard, *The Economic Consequences of the Peace* (New York: Har-
court, Brace and Howe, 1920), 298 pp.   The book that made Keynes famous is
of especial significance here in regard to its material on President Wilson.
Keynes, John Maynard, *The General Theory of Employment, Interest, and Money*
(New York: Harcourt, Brace and Company, 1936), 405 pp.   This volume should be
consulted with reference to the depression of 1929 and the attempts of the New
Deal to combat it.
Keyserling, Hermann von, *America Set Free* (New York: Harper and Brothers,
1929), 609 pp.   Possibly the most profound work ever penned on America, but its
author unfortunately becomes lost in the philosophical ionosphere at times.
Keyserling, Hermann von, *The Travel Diary of a Philosopher*, 2 volumes (New York:
Harcourt, Brace and Company, 1925), Volume I 338 pp; Volume II 400 pp.   Von
Keyserling's observations take the form of the customary travelogue, although
the philosopher broke a precedent by crossing the nation from West to East instead
of in the opposite direction.   Translated by J. Holroyd Reece.
Koht, Halvdan, *The American Spirit in Europe* (Philadelphia: University of Pennsylvania Press, 1949), 289 pp.   An important study dealing with the impact of this
country on its trans-Atlantic partner.
Lafond, Andre, *Impressions of America* (Paris: Foundation Ralph Beaver Strassburger,
1930), 207 pp.   Laford's volume was selected in 1928 by a French jury as "the most
meritorious journalistic contribution in the year 1928 to Franco-American friendship."   Translated by Lawrence Riesner.

Landau, Rom, *Among the Americans* (London: Robert Hale Limited, 1953), 219 pp. A typical book of its type which developed out of a trip that its author made to the United States in 1952.

Laski, Harold, *The American Democracy* (New York: The Viking Press, 1948), 785 pp. One of the longest, as well as most important, works ever written on America.

Laski, Harold, *The American Presidency* (New York: Harper and Brothers, 1940), 278 pp. This masterpiece was originally presented as a series of lectures at Indiana University in 1938-1939 under the auspices of the Pattan Foundation.

Laski, Harold, *Authority in the Modern State* (New Haven: Yale University Press, 1919), 398 pp. Dedicated to Felix Frankfurter and Oliver Wendell Holmes, this early Laskian study concentrates on the question of sovereignty.

Laski, Harold, *The Dangers of Obedience* (New York: Harper and Brothers, 1930), 293 pp. The most noteworthy sketch in this collection is the piece entitled "The American Political System."

Laski, Harold, *Democracy in Crisis* (Chapel Hill: The University of North Carolina Press, 1935), 267 pp. An expanded version of the Weil lectures, delivered at the University of North Carolina in 1931.

Laski, Harold, *The Dilemma of Our Times* (London: George Allen and Unwin, 1952), 272 pp. An incomplete work which was originally intended as a supplement to Laski's earlier *Faith, Reason, and Civilization*.

Laski, Harold, *A Grammar of Politics* (New Haven: Yale University Press, 1925), 672 pp. Largely theoretical in nature, this is one of its author's most extensive books.

Laski, Harold, *An Introduction to Politics* (London: George Allen and Unwin, 1954), 111 pp. Admittedly something of a popularization, *An Introduction to Politics* might best be described as a digest of the earlier *A Grammar of Politics*.

Laski, Harold, *Liberty in the Modern State* (New York: The Viking Press, 1949), 419 pp.. Here again Laski presents the case for socialism in a weighty analysis of the present era of history.

Laski, Harold, *The Strategy of Freedom* (New York: Harper and Brothers, 1941), 144 pp. Subtitled "An Open Letter to American Youth," this polemic is a plea against American isolationism.

Laski, Harold, *Trade Unions in the New Society* (New York: The Viking Press, 1949), 182 pp. An examination of American labor based on the Sidney Hillman Lectures for 1949.

Lehman, Lucien, *The American Illusion* (New York: The Century Company, 1931), 203 pp. Along with Duhamel's *America the Menace* this is one of the most significant anti-American studies. Translated by Eloise Parkhurst Huguenin.

Lewis, Wyndham, *America and Cosmic Man* (New York: Doubleday and Company, 1949), 241 pp. The main thesis of Lewis' work is that the United States is a primitive model of a new world order.

Lewis, Wyndham, *America, I Presume* (New York: Howell, Soskin and Company, 1940), 298 pp. This volume consists of impressions derived from a trip which its author made to this country around the time of the outbreak of World War II.

Madariaga, Salvador de, *I. Americans* (London: Oxford University Press, 1930) 148 pp. A collection of a number of rather short essays, the majority of which formerly appeared in the New York publication *The Forum*.

Madariaga, Salvador de, *Victors, Beware* (London: Jonathan Cape, 1946), 304 pp.

An examination of some of the problems facing liberalism in the post-World War II world.

Madariaga, Salvador de, *The World's Design* (London: George Allen and Unwin, 1938), 291 pp. A study of international politics which was written just prior to the outbreak of World War II.

Maritain, Jacques, *Reflections on America* (New York: Charles Scribner's Sons, 1958), 205 pp. An evaluation of American life based on a series of three seminars held at the University of Chicago in 1956.

Maurois, Andre, *Etats-Unis 39* (Paris: Les Editions de France, 1939), 198 pp. This book is a transcript of a diary which Maurois kept while in this nation in 1939.

Maurois, Andre, *From My Journal* (New York: Harper and Brothers, 1948), 250 pp. Another diary, this one for the year 1946. Translated by Joan Charles.

Maurois, Andre, *The Miracle of America* (New York: Harper and Brothers, 1944), 428 pp. A rather unoriginal and unimaginative history of the United States.

Maurois, Andre, *A Private Universe* (New York: D. Appleton and Company, 1932), 365 pp. Maurois presents here a collection of highly diverse essays which contains a section on America. Translated by Hamish Miles.

Mises, Ludwig von, *The Anti-Capitalistic Mentality* (Princeton: D. Van Nostrand Company, 1956), 114 pp. A defense of capitalism which involves this nation to the extent that it is the leading capitalist country in the world.

Mises, Ludwig von, *Bureaucracy* (New Haven: Yale University Press, 1944), 125 pp. Von Mises here sets forth the thesis that the battle between capitalism and socialism must end in a clear-cut victory for one side or the other.

Muller-Freienfels, Richard, *Mysteries of the Soul* (New York: Alfred A. Knopf, 1929), 348 pp. The chapter entitled "The Americanization of the Soul" is one of the most stimulating pieces ever written on this nation. Translated by Bernard Miall.

Myrdal, Gunnar, *An American Dilemma*, 2 volumes (New York: Harper and Brothers, 1944), Volume I 705 pp; Volume II 1483 pp. (paged continuously). This monumental work on the American Negro was penned between 1938 and 1942 under the auspices of the Carnegie Foundation.

Myrdal, Gunnar, *An International Economy* (New York: Harper and Brothers, 1956), 381 pp. Myrdal here writes of the conflict between the basic international economy (which includes the United States) and the economies of the newly independent nations.

Myrdal, Gunnar, *Population* (Cambridge: Harvard University Press, 1940), 237 pp. This study is based on a set of four lectures which Myrdal delivered at Harvard University in the Spring of 1938 under the auspices of the Godkin Foundation.

Namier, Lewis, *Skyscrapers and Other Essays* (London: Macmillan and Company, 1931), 183 pp. A collection of twenty essays, the first three of which deal with the United States.

Ortega y Gasset, Jose, *The Revolt of the Masses* (New York: W. W. Norton and Company, 1932), 204 pp. The most famous of Ortega y Gasset's works has little complimentary to say in regard to America, especially since Ortega y Gasset believes that this nation has allowed too much power to pass into the hands of the masses. Translated anonymously.

Riencourt, Amaury de, *The Coming Caesars* (New York: Coward-McCann, 1957), 384 pp. De Riencort here draws a parallel between ancient Rome and modern

America, but despite his efforts in the direction of originality the book has a strong Spenglerian flavor.

Romier, Lucien, *Who Will Be Master: Europe or America?* (New York: The Macauley Company, 1928), 299 pp. An important examination of American life which mixes the sweet with the bitter. Translated by Matthew Josephson.

Ropke, Wilhelm, *Crises and Cycles* (London: William Hodge and Company, 1936), 224 pp. Ropke is much closer to Schumpeter than to Keynes, and thus his remarks in regard to the depression of 1929 serve as an antidote to those expressed by the author of *The General Theory of Employment, Interest, and Money.*

Ropke, Wilhelm, *The Social Crisis of Our Time* (Chicago: University of Chicago Press, 1950), 260 pp. This impressive book analyzes the present world situation in terms of the corruption of liberalism by rationalism. Translated by Annette and Peter Jacobsohn.

Rougemont, Denis de, *Man's Western Quest* (New York: Harper and Brothers, 1957) 197 pp. A profound analysis of Western civilization in which the author takes the side of Europe rather than that of the United States or the Soviet Union.

Roussy de Sales, Raoul de, *The Making of Tomorrow* (New York: Reynal and Hitchcock, 1942), 388 pp. De Roussy de Sales' tome presents a pessimistic evaluation of the world scene in which nationalism, collectivism, and pacifism are taken to task.

Russell, Bertrand, *Freedom versus Organization 1814-1914* (New York: W. W. Norton, 1934), 471 pp. Part Three of this study is devoted to the United States, and the plutocracy Russell has discovered here.

Russell, Bertrand, *A History of Western Philosophy* (New York: Simon and Schuster, 1945), 895 pp. The chapters on William James and John Dewey are the pertinent ones in Russell's monumental work.

Russell, Bertrand, and others, *The Impact of America on European Culture* (Boston: The Beacon Press, 1951), 100 pp. Russell contributed the essay entitled "The Political and Cultural Influence" to this collection.

Russell, Bertrand, *Power* (New York: W. W. Norton and Company, 1938), 315 pp. An examination of the various forms in which power manifests itself.

Sartre, Jean-Paul, *Literary and Philosophical Essays* (New York: Criterion Books, 1955), 239 pp. These essays were selected from the author's *Situations I* and *III*, and the three dealing with America stem from Sartre's trip to the United States during World War II. Translated by Annette Michelson.

Schumpeter, Joseph, *Capitalism, Socialism, and Democracy* (New York: Harper and Brothers, 1947), 411 pp. Schumpeter here states his famous thesis that capitalism is dying and that it will be replaced eventually by socialism, although he does express his admiration for the economic system that has developed in the United States.

Shaw, George Bernard, *The Political Madhouse in America and Nearer Home* (London: Constable and Company, 1933), 63 pp. An amusing trifle which Shaw delivered as a lecture to the Academy of Political Science in New York in 1933.

Siegfried, Andre, *America at Mid-Century* (New York: Harcourt, Brace and Company, 1927), 358 pp. This key work concentrates on the ethnic, economic, and political factors in American civilization. Translated by H. H. and Doris Hemming.

Siegfried, Andre. *Nations Have Souls* (New York: G. P. Putnam's Sons, 1952), 213 pp. The section of Siegfried's volume dealing with the United States stresses the role of immigration and the racial question in American history. Translated by Edward Fitzgerald.

Siegfried, Andre, *Qu'est-ce que l'Amérique?* (Paris: Flammarion, 1937), 48 pp. Although this study is little more than a pamphlet, it still contains a great deal of important material.

Spender, J. A., *Through English Eyes* (New York: Frederick A. Stokes Company, 1928), 324 pp. Spender's book is based largely on two visits that the author made to American in 1921 and 1927-1928, and in form is part travelogue and part analysis.

Spengler, Oswald, *The Decline of the West*, 2 volumes (New York: Alfred A. Knopf, 1926-1928), Volume I 443 pp; Volume II 507 pp. Spengler's *magrum opus* contains only a limited number of references to the United States, and most of these are in Volume II. Translated by Charles Francis Atkinson.

Spengler, Oswald, *The Hour of Decision* (New York: Alfred A. Knopf, 1934), 230 pp. This polemic finds the erratic German genius in one of his more incoherent moods, especially in regard to the American scene. Translated by Charles Francis Atkinson.

Sternberg, Fritz, *Capitalism and Socialism on Trial* (New York: The John Day Company, 1951), 603 pp. Considerable emphasis is placed on the United States and Russia in this work, most of which is devoted to developments in this century. Translated by Edward Fitzgerald.

Sternberg, Fritz, *The Coming Crisis* (New York: The John Day Company, 1947), 280 pp. Sternberg's volume explores the thesis that capitalism is moving towards a period of crisis which it probably will not survive. Translated by Edward Fitzgerald.

Sternberg, Fritz, *How to Stop the Russians Without War* (New York: The John Day Company, 1948), 146 pp. A plea for a more progressive American foreign policy and for the unification of Europe. Translated by Ralph Mannheim.

Strachey, J. St. Loe, *American Soundings* (New York: D. Appleton and Company, 1926), 256 pp. This is a combination analysis and travelogue stressing both political and cultural elements.

Tardieu, Andre, *France and America* (Boston: Houghton Mifflin Company, 1927), 312 pp. Subtitled "Some Experiences in Cooperation," Tardieu's book seems to be devoted mainly to proving that a close rapport between France and the United States has been the exception rather than the rule during the last two centuries.

Teilhac, Ernest, *Pioneers of American Economic Thought in the Nineteenth Century* (New York: The Macmillan Company, 1936), 187 pp. The three major Nineteenth Century American economists dealt with are Daniel Raymond, Henry Carey, and Henry George. Translated by E. A. J. Johnson.

Thistlethwaite, Frank, *The Anglo-American Connection in the Early Nineteenth Century* (Philadelphia: University of Pennsylvania Press, 1959), 222 pp. This significant study contains in slighly altered form a series of lectures which Thistlewaite delivered at the University of Pennsylvania in 1956.

Thistlethwaite, Frank, *The Great Experiment* (Cambridge: University Press, 1955), 335 pp. A quite undistinguished history of the United States written from the British point of view.

Toynbee, Arnold, *Civilization on Trial* (New York: Oxford University Press, 1948), 203 pp. This is a series of thirteen essays, most of them dating from 1947, which stress the modern period of American history.

Toynbee, Arnold, *A Study of History*, 10 volumes (London: Oxford University Press, 1934-1954). The United States is here treated as a part of Western civilization rather than as an independent unit, and references to it are quite fragmentary.

Wallas, Graham, *Our Social Heritage* (New Haven: Yale University Press, 1921),

307 pp. Wallas emphasizes the educational system of this country in this volume.

Ward, Barbara, *Faith and Freedom* (New York: W. W. Norton and Company, 1954), 308 pp. The pertinent material on America is in parts three and four of Ward's study.

Ward, Barbara, *Policy for the West* (New York: W. W. Norton and Company, 1951), 317 pp. This work is something of a continuation of *The West at Bay*.

Ward, Barbara, *The West at Bay* (New York: W. W. Norton and Company, 1948), 248 pp. Economics plays a large role in this book, which is in essence an examination of the Western world in the post-World War II era.

Webb, Sidney and Beatrice, *The Decay of Capitalist Civilization* (London: published jointly by the Fabian Society and George Allen and Unwin, 1923), 182 pp. A tear-jerking polemic against capitalism which pictures the present economic scene in sharply defined shades of black and white.

Wells, H. G., *The Fate of Man* (New York: Longmans, Green and Company, 1939), 263 pp. Wells' extremely pessimistic lament comes to the conclusion that the problems of an increasingly complex civilization are beyond the powers of the human brain.

Wells, H. G., *The New America: The New World* (New York: The Macmillan Company, 1935), 78 pp. A rather short sketch which is essentially a study of the United States during the early days of the New Deal.

Wells, H. G., *The Outline of History*, 2 volumes (New York: The Macmillan Company, 1921), Volume I 648 pp.; Volume II 676 pp. Most of the material dealing with this nation is contained in the second of the two volumes.

Wells, H. G., *The Way the World Is Going* (New York: Doubleday, Doran and Company, 1929), 324 pp. The articles included here originally appeared in the New York *Times;* the Sacco-Vanzetti case seems to be the focal point of the sketches on the United States.

Zimmern, Alfred, *America and Europe* (New York: Oxford University Press, 1929), 213 pp. A collection of essays of which the pertinent pieces are "America and Europe" and "American Universities."

Zimmern, Alfred, *The American Road to World Peace* (New York: E. P. Dutton and Company, 1953), 287 pp. The material on the United States is concentrated in the first part of this study.

ARTICLES

Belloc, Hilaire, "The American Alliance," in *Living Age*, CCCXVII (June 9, 1923), 595-600. A criticism of the proposed Anglo-American alliance.

Belloc, Hilaire, "A Catholic View of Religious America," in *Century Magazine*, CVII (April 1924) 824-831. Belloc's article stresses the religious differences between the United States and Europe.

Beloff, Max, "Anti-Colonialism in American Foreign Policy," in *Commentary*, XXIV (September 1957), 204-211. In this piece Beloff attacks the distorted thinking of Americans in regard to colonialism.

Bonn, M. J. "America Turns Away from Europe," in *Living Age*, CCCV (June 19, 1920), 688-691. An analysis of the position of the United States in the post-World War I international scene.

Bonn, M. J., "The American Way," in *Atlantic Monthly*, CXLII (September 1928), 300-308. This sketch is brief yet important.

Bonn, M. J., "President Wilson: An Austrian View," in *Living Age*, CCC (March 1,

1919), 522-526. Bonn's essay is in general complimentary towards Wilson.

Brogan, Denis, "The Catholic Church in America," in *Harper's Magazine*, CC (May 1950), 40-50. American Popery as viewed by an English agnostic.

Brogan, Denis, "Politics and United States Foreign Policy," in *International Affairs*, XXXIII (April 1957), 165-175. The emphasis of this piece is on the Eisenhower Administration.

Fay, Bernard, "Catholic America," in *Living Age*, CCCXXXV (September 1928), 53-56. Fay's sketch tends to emphasize the strong points of the Catholic position rather than the weak ones.

Fay, Bernard, "The Course of French-American Friendship," in *Yale Review*, XVIII (March 1929), 437-455. A discussion of the obstacles to a mutual understanding between America and France.

Fay, Bernard, "Protestant America," in *Living Age*, XXXIV (August 1928), 1193-1201. This article is as hostile in its way as its companion piece on the Catholics is complimentary.

Fay, Bernard, "Psychologie du peuple americain," in *Revue des Deux Mondes*, XI (s8) September 1, 1932), 113-126. A significant essay dealing with many facets of American life.

Ferrero, Guglielmo, "America's Role in the Peace Drama," in *Living Age*, CCCVII (November 13, 1920), 377-382. The main thesis of Ferrero's article is that the United States was deprived by England and France of any action at Versailles on the question of freedom of the seas, so that there is no good reason why America should not turn its back on Europe.

Keyserling, Hermann von, "America and Germany," in *Forum*, XXXI (April 1929), 199-203. Von Keyserling here maintains that Germany and the United States are historical allies even though at times they may be enemies.

Keyserling, Hermann von, "The Animal Ideal in America," in *Harper's Magazine*, CLIX (August 1929), 265-276. This highly interesting sketch stresses the point that America has an animal ideal of existence rather than a spiritual one.

Keyserling, Hermann von, "The South—America's Hope," in *Atlantic Monthly*, CXLIV (November 1929), 605-608. A prediction that the future of the United States rests in the hands of the South.

Laski, Harold, "President Roosevelt and Foreign Opinion" in *Yale Review*, XXII (June 1933), 707-713. More of an examination of the possibilities open to F. D. R. than an evaluation of his achievements.

Laski, Harold, "The Public Papers and Addresses of Franklin D. Roosevelt," in *University of Chicago Law Bulletin*, VI (December 1938), 23-35. This book review is one of Laski's most important essays on Roosevelt.

Laski, Harold, "The Roosevelt Experiment," in *Atlantic Monthly*, CLIII (February 1934), 143-153. An analysis of F. D. R. which complements "President Roosevelt and Foreign Opinion."

Laski, Harold, "Woodrow Wilson After Ten Years," in *Forum*, LXXXV (March 1931), 129-133. This piece is surprisingly critical of Wilson and is a manifestation of the hostile climate of opinion abroad towards him.

Roussy de Sales, Raoul de, "What Makes an American," in *Atlantic Monthly*, CLXIII (March 1939), 295-304. De Roussy de Sales here contrasts rather than compares America and Europe.

Russell, Bertrand, "Can Americans and Britons be Friends," in *Saturday Evening Post*, CCXVI (June 3, 1944), 14-15 and 57-59. Russell here answers his question in the affirmative after pointing out the contrast which exists between the Old World and the New.

Russell, Bertrand, "The New Philosophy of America," in *Fortnightly Review*, CXXIX (May 1928), 618-623. A generally complimentary evaluation of present day America.

Siegfried, Andre, "America's Crisis," in *Living Age*, CCCL (June 1936), 290-300. This article is somewhat critical of the New Deal and at the same time friendly towards the business interests of the United States.

Siegfried, Andre, "L'Europe devant la civilisation américaine," in *Revue des Deux Mondes*, LVI (s7) (April 15, 1930), 757-773. A significant examination of the effect of mass production on American life.

Siegfried, Andre, "Will Europe Be Americanized," in *Yale Review*, XIX (March 1930), 433-446. Siegfried maintains here that it would be a mistake for Europe to imitate America's penchant for quantity.

Thistlethwaite, Frank, "America and Two Nations of Englishmen," in *Virginia Quarterly Review*, XXXI (Autumn 1955), 505-525. An important study which traces the trans-Atlantic relations of conservatives and liberals.

Thistlethwaite, Frank, "The Citadel and the Caravan," in *American Quarterly*, IX (Spring 1957), 22-33. Subtitled "Anglo-American Relations in the Twentieth Century," this is another significant essay by Thistlethwaite.

Toynbee, Arnold, "America, England and World Affairs," in *Harper's Magazine*, CLII (March 1926), 483-490. A rather rambling discourse on certain aspects of the American scene.

Toynbee, Arnold, "Impressions of the American State of Mind," in *International Affairs*, XIII (May-June 1934), 342-360. Toynbee here analyzes the depression of 1929 and the New Deal on the basis of a trip that he made to the United States in the Winter of 1932-1933.

INDEX

181